W9-AAI-390

AVON FREE PUBLIC LIBRARY

pipsqueak
knits

Deluxe QuickKnits for Babies & Toddlers

jil eaton

MINNOWKNITS™

Photographs by Nina Fuller

Breckling Press

AVON FREE PUBLIC LIBRARY
281 Country Club Road, Avon, CT 06001

746
.432
Eat.
c.1

Library of Congress Cataloging-in-Publication Data

Eaton, Jil, 1949-
  Pipsqueak knits : deluxe quickknits for babies & toddlers / Jil Eaton ;
photographs by Nina Fuller.
    p. cm.
  ISBN 978-1-933308-23-4
  1. Knitting--Patterns. 2. Children's clothing. I. Title.
  TT825.E28565 2008
  746.43'2041--dc22
                        2008027684

Every effort has been made to be accurate and complete with all the information in this book.
The publisher and the author cannot be responsible for differences in knitters' abilities, typographical errors, techniques, tools or conditions or any resulting damages or mistakes or losses.

Editorial direction by Anne Knudsen
Cover and interior design by Maria Mann
Photography direction and styling by Jil Eaton and Stephanie Doben
Cover and interior photographs by Nina Fuller
Pattern design by Jil Eaton
Drawings by Jil Eaton
Schematics by Stephanie Doben
Learn-to-knit illustrations by Joni Coniglio
Technical writing and editing by Stephanie Doben
Pattern proofing and editing by Janice Bye

This book was set in Century Gothic and Murray Hill
Printed in China

Published by Breckling Press, a division of Knudsen, Inc.
283 Michigan Street, Elmhurst, IL 60126, USA

Copyright © 2008 by Jennifer Lord Eaton. All rights reserved. Except as permitted under the
United States Copyright Act of 1976, no part of this publication may be reproduced or distributed
in any form or by any means, or stored in a database or retrieval system, without the prior written
permission of the publisher. Commercial use of this publication and its contents is strictly prohibited.

International Standard Book Number: 978-1-933308-23-4

Minnowknits hand-knitting patterns may not be knit for re-sale. Minnowknits are trademarked and copyrighted
under US and international law by Jennifer Lord Eaton, Small Pond Studios, 52 Neal Street, Portland, Maine 04102,
USA (www.minnowknits.com). All rights reserved. No copies of any or all of
this publication may be made without the express written permission of the publisher and author.
MinnowKnits™ patterns and books and MinnowMerino™ yarns are distributed by Classic Elite Yarns, 125 Western
Avenue, Lowell, MA 01851 (www.classiceliteyarns.com).

Dedication

*To Stephanie Doben, my studio and design assistant, technical
pattern writer and editor, stylist, graphic designer, fabulous
knitter, model scout and lovely friend.*

Contents

babies

Baby, Baby, Baby!

Ah, babies. Our little bundles of joy and energy, lighting up our lives day by day. When it comes to discovering luxury for your baby or toddler, look no further than your own knitting basket. Start with an array of sumptuous yarns in saturated colors and blends, and whip up some darling confections. Return to the classics, such as an adorable baby layette, but add the modern twist of detailed design and chic styling. Babies deserve the very best, heirloom quality garments in creamy cashmere, soft, soft merino, silks and blends or fluffy kid mohair. Warm and soft in your hands and on your babies, these inimitable fibers make knitting for your baby a pleasure.

Jil Eaton

This *Pipsqueaks Knits* collection mixes delightful classics touched with true whimsy and unique details. Sweaters and sleepsuits, carriage blankets and companion caps, rompers and jackets, snowsuits and dresses, all chic and charming for your own precious tyke. Luxury is key in these unexpected projects, characterized by plush panache where comfort and style are one. And knowing how hectic life can be, these projects are my trademark QuickKnits, which you can knit up in a jiffy!

Always, always knit with the highest quality yarns you can find; the time investment, even on a tiny baby project, warrants the best in materials. And always look for the most beautiful colors and fibers. Most natural fibers are best, as the fibers breathe and are wonderful in your hands. They wear beautifully, too—perfect for your baby projects.

Remember, when we are knitting, all is right with the world . . .

Jil Eaton

Knitting to Fit

From newborn on up, babies are a delight to knit for. But little ones grow faster than you can imagine, so the trick is to finish each garment in time for your baby or toddler to get plenty of wear out of it. To make sure your finished garments fit comfortably, pay close attention to the following preparatory steps.

getting the gauge

The single most important step when beginning any knitting project is to do a gauge swatch. The gauge swatch is a 4"/10 cm square, knit in the pattern called for and with the recommended needle size. Getting the correct gauge, or number of stitches per inch, allows you to make a fabric that is even and smooth, with the correct drape and hand, resulting in the correct size. Any garment that is off the gauge one stitch per inch may end up five inches too big or small! Simply doing your gauge swatch will insure a happy result, every time. It also can become part of your knitting history, and is perfect for testing washability and felting.

Using the needles suggested in the pattern, cast on the correct number of stitches to make a 4"/10 cm swatch, plus six more stitches. Knit three rows. Always knit three stitches at the beginning and end of every row, and work straight in

the pattern stitches called for until the piece measures 4"/10 cm. Knit three more rows and bind off. Lay the swatch on a flat, smooth surface. Measure inside the garter stitch frame; you should have 4"/10 cm exactly. If your swatch is too big, or you have too few stitches per inch, change to a needle one size smaller. If your swatch is too small, or there are too many stitches per inch, change to the next largest needles. Getting into the habit of doing your gauge swatch will fine-tune your craftsmanship, making you a better knitter for life.

Knitting Kit

A clear zippered case is best for the perfect knitting kit. Everything is visible and it's easy to fish out items you need. If you set yourself up with the following items, you have a portable studio, easily stashed in your knitting bag.

* *Small, very sharp scissors, used only for yarn.*
* *Yarn needles: I like the Japanese Chibi needles with bent tips.*
* *Cable needles: I use straight US sizes 3, 6 and 10.*
* *Retractable measuring tape.*
* *Yarn T-pins and yarn safety pins for marking or holding dropped stitches.*

how to measure your pipsqueak

My silhouette is generous, with room for easy dressing and comfortable movement. Measure your child carefully, and go to the next biggest size. And remember that babies grow at an alarming rate, so keep that in mind when choosing your size.

A: Measure around the widest part of the head, above the ears.

B: CBS or center-back-sleeve. Measure from the middle of the back straight to the wrist, with the arms outstretched.

C: Around the chest, just under the arms

D: Around the waist.

E: Shoulder to waist or torso length.

F: Waist to knee, for tunics, dresses, or longer sweaters.

caring for handknits

Once you have finished knitting, block each piece of the garment so that it retains its shape. Cover each piece with two damp towels, one under and one over, pinning pieces in place. Or pin to a blocking board. Lightly steam at the appropriate setting for the yarn you are using, and dry your garment flat on a towel, mesh

rack, or on the blocking board. Blocking usually improves the look of your garment, as long as it is gently done.

You will want to launder your baby sweaters, and your gauge swatches are absolutely perfect for testing the washability of a specific yarn, following the yarn label instructions. Most yarns are machine washable. Place the garment in a small mesh bag (to hold its shape), then set the machine on a very gentle cycle in tepid water. This will get your garment really clean. You should use a no-rinse sweater soap such as Eucalan, which is available at fine yarn shops as well as on the Internet. And there are now wonderful "superwash" yarns, but use a gentle laundry soap on those, not the no-rinse products as they will ruin your garment!

* Stitch holders, both long and short. English Aeros are my favorites, but Japanese holders that are open at either end are also fabulous.

* Stitch markers: split-rings are good as they can be easily moved and removed.

* Point protectors, both large and small, to keep your work on the needles.

* Needle/gauge ruler—essential.

* Crochet hooks: one small, one large.

* Dentists' tool, with one hooked end and one smooth end— invaluable.

* Pen and small notebook, for notes, figuring, and design notes.

* Small calculator, which you will use constantly.

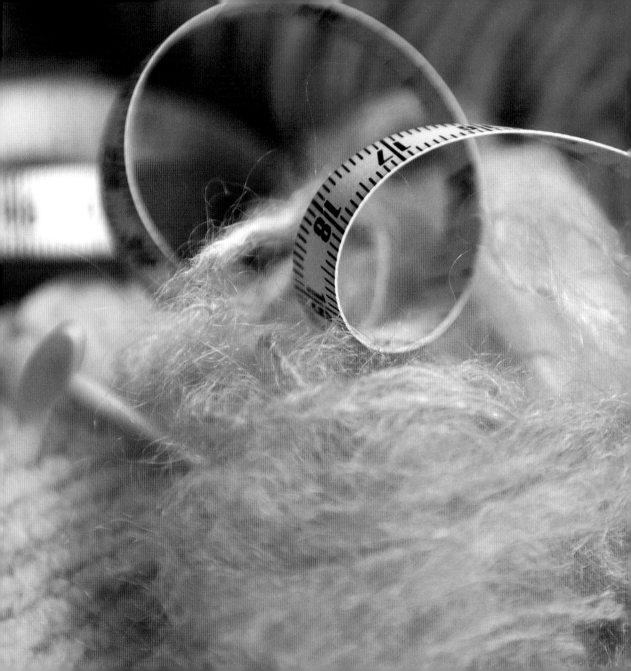

Learn to Knit

This learn-to-knit section takes you through the basic elements of knitting. Although there are many others, I have included only two types of cast-ons, the *knit-on cast-on* and the *cable cast-on*. Once you have mastered the knit-on method, you have actually learned the basic knit stitch. The cable cast-on is a variation on the same stitch and is used to form a sturdy, yet elastic edge.

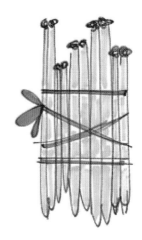

slip knot

1 Hold the yarn in your left hand, leaving a short length free. Wrap the yarn from the skein into a circle and bring the yarn from below and up through the center of the circle. Insert the needle under this strand as shown.

2 Pull on both the short and long ends to tighten the knot on the needle.

Step 1 Slip Knot

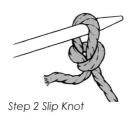

Step 2 Slip Knot

knit-on cast-on

1   Hold the needle with the slip-knot in the left hand and the empty needle in the right hand. Insert the right needle from front to back under the left needle and through the stitch. With the yarn in the right hand, wrap the yarn around the right needle as shown.

2   With the tip of the right needle, pull the wrap through the stitch on the left needle and bring to the front.

3   Slip the new stitch off the right needle and onto the left needle. Repeat steps 1 to 3 for a simple knit-on cast-on.

Step 1 Knit-On Cast-On

Step 2 Knit-On Cast-On

Step 3 Knit-On Cast-On

cable cast-on

1   Work Steps 1 and 2 of the knit-on cast-on above. Insert the right needle between the first two stitches on the left needle and wrap the yarn around the needle as shown.

2   With the tip of the right needle, pull the wrap through to the front.

3   Slip the new stitch off the right needle and onto the left needle. Repeat Steps 1 to 3 for a cable cast-on.

Step 1 Cable Cast-On

basic knit stitch

1   Hold the needle with the cast-on stitches in the left hand and hold the empty needle in the right hand. Insert the right needle from front to back into the first stitch on the left needle and wrap the yarn just as in the first step of the cast-on.

Step 1 Basic Knit Stitch

2   With the tip of the right needle, pull the wrap through the stitch on the left needle and onto the right needle. Drop the stitch from the left needle. A new stitch is made on the right needle. Repeat steps 1 and 2 until all the stitches from the left needle are on the right needle. Turn the work and hold the needle with the new stitches in the left hand and continue knitting.

Step 2 Basic Knit Stitch

Step 1 Basic Purl Stitch

basic purl stitch

The purl stitch is the opposite of the knit stitch. Instead of pulling the wrapped yarn towards you, you will push it through the back of the stitch. Because it is harder to see what you are doing, the purl stitch is a bit harder to learn than the knit stitch.

1   Hold the needle with the cast-on stitches in the left hand and the empty needle in the right hand. Insert the right needle from back to front, into the first stitch on the left needle, and wrap the yarn counter-clockwise around the needle as shown.

2   With the tip of the right needle, pull the wrap through the stitch on the left needle and onto the right needle, as in the knit stitch. Drop the stitch from the left needle. A new stitch is made on the right needle. Continue in this way across the row.

stockinette stitch

On straight needles, knit on the right side, purl on the wrong side. On a circular needle, knit every row.

garter stitch

When knitting with straight needles, knit every row. On a circular needle, knit one row, purl one row.

decrease or knit two together (k2tog)

Hold the needle with the knitted fabric in the left hand and hold the empty needle in the right hand. Insert the right needle from front to back through the first two stitches on the left needle. Wrap the yarn and pull through the two stitches as if knitting. Drop the two stitches from the left needle. One new stitch is made from two stitches; therefore one stitch is decreased.

Knit Two Together

increase

Knit in the front of the stitch, and, without removing the stitch from the left hand needle, knit in the back of the same stitch, then drop the stitches from the left needle. This makes two stitches in one stitch.

bind off

Hold the needle with the knitting in the left hand and hold the empty needle in the right hand. Knit the first two stitches. * With the left needle in front of the right needle, insert the tip of the left needle into the second stitch on the right needle and pull it over the first stitch and off the right needle. One stitch has been bound off. Knit the next stitch, then repeat from the * until all the stitches are bound off.

Bind Off

Puddlejumper

Love those stripes! This playful multi-colored romper has clever leg-band buttons for easy changing. With long legs and long sleeves, your tot will be toasty warm and ready to play!

- **beginner quickknit**

sizes

3–6 months (6–12 months, 12–18 months)
Finished chest: 19½ (22, 24)"/50 (56, 61) cm
Finished length, shoulder to ankle: 19 (22½, 25½)"/48 (57, 64.5) cm

materials

Worsted weight yarn: 270 (350, 430) yards/250 (320, 395) meters in A; 85 (115, 140) yards/80 (105, 130) meters each in B and C
Straight needles: Sizes 7 and 8 US (4.5 and 5 mm)
Circular needle, 24"/61 cm: Size 8 US (5 mm)
Stitch holders and markers
Four 7/8"/2.25 cm buttons for shoulders
Five (seven, seven) ¾"/2 cm buttons for legs

gauge

18 sts and 24; rows = 4"/10 cm over St st using larger needles

✓ *Always check gauge to save time and ensure a perfect fit. Adjust needle size as necessary.*

pipsqueak profile

model: *Elliot, but my nickname is Elbow*

hobby: *Standing on my head*

loves: *Daddy anything*

hates: *Car rides*

favorite stuffie: *Duckie*

Photographed in Jil Eaton MinnowMerino (50g/77yds): #4757 Bluette (A), #4720 Aqua Aqua (B) and #4758 Rouge (C). Sample knit by Pam Tessier.

Stripe Patterns

(Worked in Stockinette st)

Stripe Pattern 1
8 rows B, 2 rows C;
repeat these 10 rows

Stripe Pattern 2
8 rows C, 2 rows A;
repeat these 10 rows

Stripe Pattern 3
8 rows A, 2 rows B;
repeat these 10 rows

back

1 **Left leg:** With smaller needles and C, cast on 18 (18, 22) sts. Work in k2, p2 rib for 1"/2.5 cm, ending with a WS row. Change to larger needles and work 3 (4, 5) repeats of Stripe Pattern 1, and *at the same time*, increase 1 st at each edge every fourteenth row 2 (0, 3) times, then every eighth row 0 (4, 0) times—22 (26, 28) sts. End with row 10 of Stripe Pattern 1. Place sts on a holder.

2 **Right leg:** With smaller needles and A, cast on 18 (18, 22) sts. Work in k2, p2 rib for 1"/2.5 cm, ending with a WS row. Change to larger needles and work 2 (3, 4) repeats plus the first 8 rows of Stripe Pattern 2, and *at the same time*, work increases as for the left leg. **Next row (RS):** With B, knit. **Next row:** With B, purl. Leave sts on needle.

3 **Join legs:** With larger needles and A, k 22 (26, 28) sts from the right leg. Cast on 5 sts, then k 22 (26, 28) sts from the left leg from the holder—49 (57, 61) sts.

4 **Body:** Beginning with row 2 of Stripe Pattern 3, work 7 (8, 9) repeats plus the first 7 rows of the pattern, and *at the same time*, decrease 1 st at each edge every eighth (sixth, sixth) row 3 (4, 4) times—43 (49, 53) sts. **Next row (WS):** With A, p 14 (16, 17), then join a second ball of A and bind off the center 15 (17, 19) sts for the back neck. Purl to the end. Working both sides at the same time with separate balls of yarn, purl 1 row (RS) for the shoulder ridge. Starting with a purl row, continue in St st for 7 more rows for the button plackets. Bind off sts.

front

5 Legs: Work the right leg as for the back and place the sts on a holder. Work the left leg as for the back and leave the sts on the needle. **Join legs:** With larger needles and A, k 22 (26, 28) sts from the left leg, the cast on 5 sts, k 22 (26, 28) sts from the right leg (from holder)—49 (57, 61) sts.

6 Body: Beginning with row 2 of Stripe Pattern 3, work 6 (7, 8) repeats plus the first 7 rows of the pattern, and *at the same time*, decrease 1 st at each edge every eighth (sixth, sixth) row 3 (4, 4) times—43 (49, 53) sts.

7 Shape neck, next row (WS): P 17 (20, 21), join the second ball of yarn and bind off 9 (9, 11) sts, then p to end. Continue in Stripe Pattern 3, working both sides at the same time with separate balls of yarn, and bind off 2 sts from the neck edge once, then decrease 1 st at each neck edge every RS row 1 (2, 2) times—14 (16, 17) sts remain on each side. Work 5 (3, 3) more rows even.

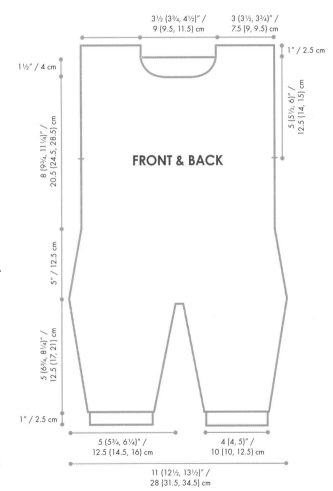

3½ (3¾, 4½)" / 9 (9.5, 11.5) cm

3 (3½, 3¾)" / 7.5 (9, 9.5) cm

1" / 2.5 cm

1½" / 4 cm

5 (5½, 6)" / 12.5 (14, 15) cm

8 (9¾, 11¼)" / 20.5 (24.5, 28.5) cm

FRONT & BACK

5" / 12.5 cm

5 (6¾, 8¼)" / 12.5 (17, 21) cm

1" / 2.5 cm

5 (5¾, 6¼)" / 12.5 (14.5, 16) cm

4 (4, 5)" / 10 (10, 12.5) cm

11 (12½, 13½)" / 28 (31.5, 34.5) cm

8 **Buttonholes, next row (WS):** Left side—k 4 (6, 7), k2tog, yo, k4, k2tog, yo, k2; right side—k2, yo, k2tog, k4, yo, k2tog, k 4 (6, 7). Work 1 more row even. Bind off sts. Sew four buttons to the shoulder button plackets opposite the buttonholes.

right sleeve

9 Place markers 5 (5½, 6)"/12.5 (14, 15) cm down from the shoulder seams. With larger needles and B pick up and knit 46 (50, 54) sts between the markers, working through both layers of button plackets. Beginning with row 2, work in St st, alternating 6 rows of B and 6 rows of C, and *at the same time*, decrease 1 st at each edge every fourth row 4 (6, 8) times, then every other row 6 (4, 4) times—26 (30, 30) sts. Work until you have finished row 6 of stripes.

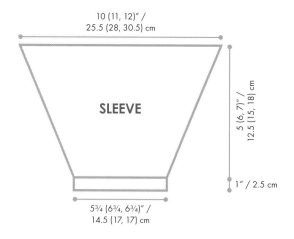

10 (11, 12)" /
25.5 (28, 30.5) cm

SLEEVE

5 (6, 7)" /
12.5 (15, 18) cm

1" / 2.5 cm

5¾ (6¾, 6¾)" /
14.5 (17, 17) cm

10 Change to smaller needles and C (B, C), then work in k2, p2 rib for 1"/2.5 cm. Bind off loosely and evenly in rib.

left sleeve

11 Work as for the right sleeve, working stripes in C and A and cuff in A (C, A).

finishing

12 Sew the side and sleeve seams. With RS facing, using a crochet hook and A, work 1 row of single crochet around the front and back neck edges.

leg button plackets

13 **Back**: With RS facing, a circular needle and A, begin at the inside bottom of the left leg pick up and k 24 (31, 38) sts along the left leg, pick up and k 5 sts across cast on sts, and pick up and k 24 (31, 38) sts down the inside of the right leg— 53 (67, 81) sts. Work in Garter st (knit every row) for 8 rows. Bind off sts. **Front**: Pick up sts as for the back. Work 4 rows in Garter st. **Buttonholes, next row (RS)**: K 2 (3, 1), yo, k2tog, [k 10 (8, 11), yo, k2tog] 4 (6, 6) times, then k 1 (2, 0). Knit 3 more rows. Bind off sts.

14 Sew 5 (7, 7) buttons to the leg button plackets opposite the buttonholes.

Cable Cutie

*Let it snow! This classic pullover will keep your tot
cozy warm all winter long. Top it with a pompom
hat, and baby is set to go. Worsted weight yarn
knits up like a dream, for a soft, wide cable.*

● ● ● **intermediate beginner**

sizes

3-6 months (1, 3) years
Sweater, finished chest: 19½ (24, 28½)"/50 (58.5, 72.5) cm
Sweater, finished length: 10 (12, 14)"/25.5 (30.5, 35.5) cm
Hat, finished circumference: 16 (18, 20)"/40.5 (45.5, 51) cm

materials

*Worsted weight yarn: 300 (425, 620) yards/275 (390, 570) meters
in MC for sweater; 85 (110, 135) yards/80 (100, 125) meters in
MC, plus 25 yards/25 meters in CC for hat*
Straight needles: Size 9 US (5.5 mm)
Cable needle (cn)
Stitch holders and markers
Crochet hook: Size H-8 (5 mm)
Double-pointed needles (dpns), set of three: Size 9 US (5.5 mm)
Three ½"/1.5 cm buttons

gauge

20 sts and 26 rows = 4"/10 cm over pattern stitch

 *Always check gauge to save time and ensure a perfect fit. Adjust
needle size as necessary.*

pipsquea**k**
profile

model: *Libby, aka Beans*

tunes: *Indie dance hits*

hobby: *I like to yell "Hey
Baby" when I see my
reflection*

loves: *Raspberries on
my belly*

hates: *Being told "No"*

favorite word: *Cheerios!*

*Photographed in Manos del
Uruguay (100g/138yds): #43
Juniper (MC); Sample knit by
Nita Young. Shoulder buttons by
Zecca add a spark of color.*

Sweater Cable Pattern

(Multiple of 11 sts plus 5)

Rows 1, 3 and 5 (RS) K1, [p1, k1] twice, *k6, [k1, p1] twice, k1; repeat from * to end

Rows 2, 4, 6 and 8 (WS) *K1, [p1, k1] twice, p6; repeat from *, end [k1, p1] twice, k1

Row 7 K1, [p1, k1] twice, *sl 3 sts to cn and hold to back, k3, k3 from cn, [k1, p1] twice, k1; repeat from * to end

Repeat rows 1-8 for pattern stitch

sweater back

1 With straight needles and MC, cast on 49 (60, 71) sts. Work in Sweater Cable Pattern until the piece measures 10 (12, 14)"/25.5 (30.5, 35.5) cm from the beginning, ending with a WS row.

2 **Next row**: Work 16 (20, 24) sts in pattern and place them on a holder for the back right shoulder. Bind off the next 17 (20, 23) sts for the back neck, then work in pattern to the end.

3 **Buttonband**: On the remaining 16 (20, 24) sts, k all rows for 1"/2.5 cm. Bind off sts.

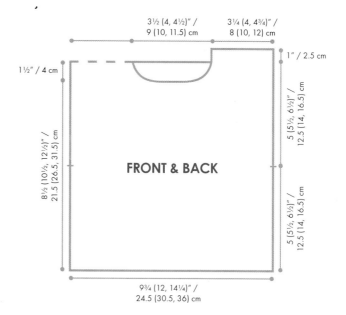

3½ (4, 4½)" / 9 (10, 11.5) cm

3¼ (4, 4¾)" / 8 (10, 12) cm

1" / 2.5 cm

1½" / 4 cm

5 (5½, 6½)" / 12.5 (14, 16.5) cm

FRONT & BACK

8½ (10½, 12½)" / 21.5 (26.5, 31.5) cm

5 (5½, 6½)" / 12.5 (14, 16.5) cm

9¾ (12, 14¼)" / 24.5 (30.5, 36) cm

sweater front

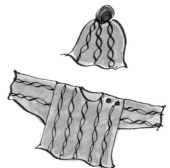

4 Work as for the back until the piece measures 8½ (10½, 12½)"/21.5 (26.5, 31.5) cm from the beginning, ending with a WS row.

5 **Shape neck, next row (RS)**: Keeping to pattern, work 20 (25, 30) sts. Join a second ball of yarn and bind off the next 9 (10, 11) sts; work to the end. Working both sides at the same time with separate balls of yarn, bind off from each neck edge 2 sts 2 (2, 3) times, then decrease 1 st each at neck edge next RS row 0 (1, 0) time. Work even on 16 (20, 24) sts each side until the piece measures 9¾ (11¾, 13¾)"/24.5 (30, 35) cm from the beginning, ending with a WS row.

6 **Buttonholes, next row (RS)**: Left shoulder—work 3 (5, 7) sts, yo, k2tog, [work 3 (4, 5) sts, yo, k2tog] twice, work 1 st. Right shoulder— with the other ball, work the remaining sts in pattern. Work 1 more row in pattern. Bind off the left shoulder sts. Leave the right shoulder sts on the needle.

knitted shoulder seam

7 With the *wrong* sides facing each other, and the front of the sweater facing you, place sts of the back and front right shoulders on two parallel dpns. The seam will be visible on the RS of the sweater. **Work three-needle bind off as follows:** With a third dpn, k the first stitch from the front needle together with the first stitch from the back needle, *k the next stitch from the front and back needles together, slip the first st over the second st to bind off; repeat from * until all sts are bound off. Cut the yarn and pull the end through the loop.

sleeves

8 With straight needles and MC, cast on 27 (27, 38) sts. Work in Sweater Cable Pattern until the sleeve measures 6 (7½, 10¼)"/15 (19, 26) cm or the desired length from the beginning, ending with a WS row. *At the same time*, increase 1 st at each edge every sixth row 0 (0, 5) times, then every fourth row 6 (8, 8) times, then every second row 6 (6, 0) times, working the increases into the pattern—51 (55, 64) sts. Bind off sts.

finishing

9 Sew on buttons.

10 Place markers 5 (5½, 6½)"/12.5 (14, 16.5) cm down from the shoulder seams and sew the sleeves between the markers. Sew the sleeve and side seams.

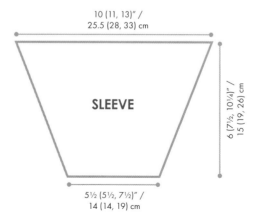

10 (11, 13)" /
25.5 (28, 33) cm

SLEEVE

6 (7½, 10¼)" /
15 (19, 26) cm

5½ (5½, 7½)" /
14 (14, 19) cm

11 With RS facing, a crochet hook and MC, begin at the left front and work 1 row of single crochet around the neck edge.

hat

1 With MC and straight needles, cast on 78 (89, 100) sts. Work in Hat Cable Pattern for 5 (5¾, 6½)"/12.5 (14.5, 16.5) cm, ending with a WS row.

2 Shape crown, next row (RS): Work 7 sts in pattern, *k1, p3tog, k1, work 6 sts in pattern; repeat from *, end k1, p3tog, k1—64 (73, 82) sts. Work 3 rows even. **Next row (RS)**: Work 7 sts in pattern, *k3tog, work 6 sts in pattern; repeat from *, end k3tog—50 (57, 64) sts. Work 1 row even. **Next row (RS)**: K2tog across, end k 0 (1, 0)—25 (29, 32) sts. **Next row** (WS): P2tog across, end p 1 (1, 0)—13 (15, 16) sts. **Next row (RS)**: K2tog across, end k 1 (1, 0). Cut the yarn, leaving an 18"/45.5 cm tail, and pull through the remaining 7 (8, 8) sts.

3 Sew the back seam.

pompom

4 Wrap CC 100 times around four fingers. Remove your fingers, then wrap 12"/30.5 cm strand of yarn twice around the center. Pull snug and tie. Cut the loops and trim the ends to form a pompom. Attach the pompom firmly to the top of the hat with the 12"/30.5 cm strand of yarn.

Hat Cable Pattern

(Multiple of 11 sts plus 1)

Rows 1, 3 and 5 (RS) K1 *k6, [k1, p1] twice, k1; repeat from * to end

Rows 2, 4, 6 and 8 (WS) *K1, [p1, k1] twice, p6; repeat from *, end p1

Row 7 K1, *sl 3 sts to cn and hold to back, k3, k3 from cn, [k1, p1] twice, k1; repeat from * to end

Repeat rows 1-8 for pattern stitch

Criss Cross

uniquely styled cardigan with shaped front edges

An unusual shaping in a soft fleecy yarn, this cardigan is a showstopper. Two Fimo buttons from the inimitable Zecca Buttons add the perfect finish.

- **beginner quickknit**

sizes

6 months (1, 2, 3) years
Finished chest (buttoned): 22 (24, 26, 28)"/56 (61, 66, 71) cm
Finished length: 10 (12, 13, 14)"/25.5 (30.5, 33, 35.5) cm

materials

Chenille yarn: 190 (230, 280, 340) yards/175 (210, 260, 315) meters
Straight needles: Size 9 US (5.5 mm)
Double pointed needles (dpns), set of three: Size 9 US (5.5 mm)
Crochet hook: Size H-8 (5 mm)
Stitch holders and markers
Two ⁷/₈"/2.25 cm buttons

gauge

12 sts and 26 rows = 4"/10 cm in Stockinette st (St st)

✓ *Always check gauge to save time and ensure a perfect fit. Adjust needle size as necessary.*

pipsqueak profile

model: *Zoë or "The Zoester"*

yummies: *Applesauce*

tunes: *Hard rock*

loves: *Playing with water*

hates: *Getting my hair done*

favorite word: *Binky*

Photographed in Knit One Crochet Too Fleece (50g/109yds): #325 Mango. Sample knit by Eroica Hunter

back

1 With straight needles, cast on 33 (36, 39, 42) sts. Work in Garter st (knit every row) for 4 rows.

2 Change to St st and work even until the piece measures 10 (12, 13, 14)" / 25.5 (30.5, 33, 35.5) cm from the beginning, ending with a WS row.

3 **Next row (RS):** K 10 (11, 12, 13) sts and place sts on a holder for the back right shoulder; bind off 13 (14, 15, 16) sts for the back neck; k to end and place sts on another holder for the back left shoulder.

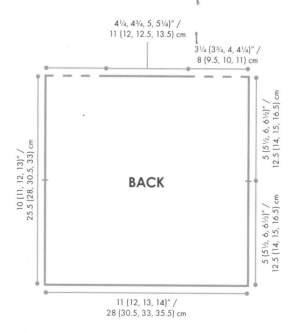

4¼, 4¾, 5, 5¼)" /
11 (12, 12.5, 13.5) cm

3¼ (3¾, 4, 4¼)" /
8 (9.5, 10, 11) cm

5 (5½, 6, 6½)" /
12.5 (14, 15, 16.5) cm

10 (11, 12, 13)" /
25.5 (28, 30.5, 33) cm

BACK

5 (5½, 6, 6½)" /
12.5 (14, 15, 16.5) cm

11 (12, 13, 14)" /
28 (30.5, 33, 35.5) cm

right front

1 With straight needles, cast on 11 (12, 13, 14) sts. Work in Garter st for 5 rows.

2 Starting with a WS (purl) row, work in St st and increase 1 st at the beginning of every sixth row 0 (1, 2, 3) times, then every fourth row 8 (12, 12, 12) times, then every second row 4 (0, 0, 0) times—23 (25, 27, 29) sts. Work even until the piece measures 8 (10, 11, 12)"/20.5 (25.5, 28, 30.5) cm from the beginning, ending with a WS row.

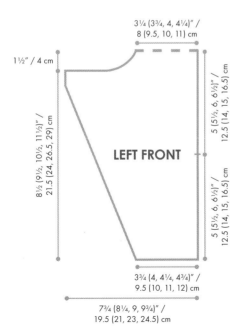

3¼ (3¾, 4, 4¼)" / 8 (9.5, 10, 11) cm

1½" / 4 cm

5 (5½, 6, 6½)" / 12.5 (14, 15, 16.5) cm

8½ (9½, 10½, 11½)" / 21.5 (24, 26.5, 29) cm

LEFT FRONT

5 (5½, 6, 6½)" / 12.5 (14, 15, 16.5) cm

3¾ (4, 4¼, 4¾)" / 9.5 (10, 11, 12) cm

7¾ (8¼, 9, 9¾)" / 19.5 (21, 23, 24.5) cm

3 **Buttonholes, next row (RS)**: K1, bind off 2 sts, k 7 (8, 9, 10), bind off 2 sts, then k to end. **Next row:** Cast on 2 sts above the bound off sts. Work 2 more rows in St st.

4 **Shape neck, next row (RS)**: Bind off 10 (11, 12, 13) sts from the neck edge once, 2 sts from the neck edge once, then decrease 1 st from the neck edge once. Work even on the remaining 10 (11, 12, 13) sts until the front is the same length as the back. Place sts on a holder for the right front shoulder.

left front

5 Work as for the right front, reversing increases and neck shaping and omitting the buttonholes. Leave sts on the needle.

shoulder seams

6 With *wrong* sides facing each other, and the front of the sweater facing you, place sts of the back and front left shoulders on two parallel dpns. The seam will be visible on the RS of the sweater. **Work three-needle bind off as follows**: With a third dpn, k the first stitch from the front needle together with the first stitch from the back needle, *k the next stitch from the front and back needles together, slip the first st over the second st to bind off; repeat from * until all sts are bound off. Cut the yarn and pull the end through the loop. Repeat for the right side.

sleeves

7 Place markers on the front and back 5 (5½, 6, 6½)"/12.5 (14, 15, 16.5) cm down from the shoulder seams.

8 With RS facing and straight needles, pick up and k 30 (33, 36, 39) sts between the markers.

9 Working in St st, decrease 1 st each edge every eighth row 0 (0, 4, 5) times, then every sixth row 5 (6, 1, 2) times, then every fourth row 1 (1, 3, 2) times— 18 (19, 20, 21) sts. Work even, if necessary, until the sleeve measures 5¾ (6¾, 8¼, 9¾)"/14.5 (17, 21, 24.5) cm, ending with a RS row.

10 Work in Garter st for 4 rows. Bind off sts loosely and evenly.

finishing

11 With RS facing and a crochet hook, work 1 row of single crochet around the neck.

12 Lap the right front over the left and sew buttons to the left front opposite the buttonholes.

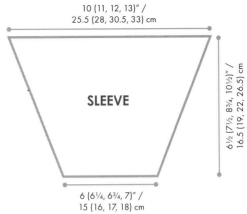

10 (11, 12, 13)" / 25.5 (28, 30.5, 33) cm

SLEEVE

6½ (7½, 8¾, 10½)" / 16.5 (19, 22, 26.5) cm

6 (6¼, 6¾, 7)" / 15 (16, 17, 18) cm

Bobbles

Take it to the streets! This carriage blanket with matching chapeau will captivate the young mother set. The blanket is great for peek-a-boo, too! With pretty bobble detailing, the project is fast to knit and makes a darling shower gift.

● ● ● ● **advanced beginner quickknit**

sizes

Blanket, finished size: 25" x 30"/63.5 x 76 cm

Hat, 3 (6, 12) months

Hat, finished circumference: 14 (16, 18)"/35.5 (40.5, 45.5) cm

materials

Sport weight yarn: 1,020 yards/935 meters for blanket; 115 (130, 145) yards/105 (120, 135) meters for hat

Circular needle, 26"/66 cm: Size 9 US (5.5 mm)

Double pointed needles (dpns), set of five: Size 9 US (5.5 mm)

gauge

16 sts and 32 rows = 4"/10 cm over Garter stitch with two strands held together

✔ *Always check gauge to save time and ensure a perfect fit. Adjust needle size as necessary.*

pipsqueak profile

model: *Artemisia, or Misia for short*

hobby: *I like to fit all ten toes in my mouth at once*

loves: *Moving and grooving to music from Madonna*

hates: *Fluoride drops*

favorite stuffie: *Conti the cat*

Photographed in Classic Elite Yarns Miracle (50g/108yds): #3329 Fundy Bay Blue. Sample knit by Nita Young

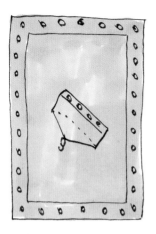

bobble blanket

1 With two strands held together and a circular needle, cast on 99 sts. **Rows 1—6**: Work in Garter st (knit every row). **Row 7 (RS)**: K4, MB, [k9, MB] 9 times, k4. **Rows 8—22**: Work in Garter st.

2 **Row 23 (RS)**: K4, MB, k to last 5 sts, MB, k4. **Rows 24—25**: Knit. **Row 26**: K12, p74, k12. **Row 27**: Knit. **Rows 28—38**: Continue as established, keeping the first and last 12 sts in Garter st and the center 74 sts in Stockinette st (St st).

3 **Row 39 (RS) (bobble row)**: K4, MB, k7, p74, k7, MB, k4. **Rows 40—165**: Continue as established and work a bobble row every sixteenth row, 7 times more. Continue in pattern as established for 14 rows more.

4 **Row 166 (WS)**: Knit. **Row 167**: K4, MB, k to last 5 sts, MB, k4. **Rows 168—182**: Work in Garter st. **Row 183 (RS)**: K4, MB, [k9, MB] 9 times, k4. **Rows 184—189**: Work in Garter st. Bind off sts. Weave in all loose ends.

Make Bobble (MB)

Knit into front, back, front, back and front of stitch—5 sts made. *Turn the work and purl these five sts; turn the work and knit five. Repeat from *. With the left needle, pull the second, third, fourth and fifth sts one at a time over the first stitch and off the needle; pull tight.

bobble hat

1 With two strands held together and dpns, cast on 4 sts.

Work I-cord as follows: K4 sts. *Do not turn the work. Slide sts to the other end of the needle to work the next row from the RS and k4; repeat from * for 1"/2.5 cm. Increase 1 st in each st on the next row to 8 sts. Divide sts evenly on 4 dpns (2 sts on each needle). Join and work in rounds of St st (k every round), increase 1 st at the end of every needle every round (therefore, 4 sts increased every round) until there are 56 (64, 72) sts, or 14 (16, 18) sts on each needle.

2 Work in Garter st (knit 1 round, purl 1 round on circular needle) for 14 (16, 16) rounds.

3 Next round: K4, MB, [k7, MB] 6 (7, 8) times, k3. Beginning with a purl round, continue in Garter st for 6 rounds more. Bind off sts knitwise. Weave in all loose ends.

Ski Ticket

super quickknit snowsuit with button closure and mitten finishing

Your little one will be the talk of the ski slopes swaddled in this winter delight. Use only the softest of yarns to keep baby snug even on the coldest days. This super bulky yarn is knit in a tight gauge for an always warm snowsuit.

- **beginner super quickknit**

sizes

3 (6, 9) months
Finished chest: 26 (28, 30)"/66 (71, 16) cm
Finished length, shoulder to foot: 19 (22, 25)"/48 (56, 63.5) cm

materials

Super bulky weight yarn (MC): 375 (470, 555) yards/345 (430, 510) meters
Worsted weight yarn (CC): 25 yards/25 meters
Straight needles: Size 13 US (9 mm)
Stitch holders and markers
Double pointed needles (dpns), set of three: Size 13 US (9 mm)
Four 1"/2.5 cm buttons

gauge

9 sts and 13 rows = 4"/10 cm over Stockinette stitch (St st)

✓ *Always check gauge to save time and ensure a perfect fit. Adjust needle size as necessary.*

pipsqueak profile

model: Daniel or Danny

tunes: Mozart

hobby: I like to wiggle my nose like a rabbit

loves: My cell phone

hates: Moisturizer

Photographed in Classic Elite Yarns Aspen (100g/51yds): #1555 Ski Ticket (MC) and Jil Eaton MinnowMerino (50g/77yds): #4720 Aqua Aqua (CC). Sample knit by Noella Kingsley.

back

1 **Left leg**: With straight needles and MC, cast on 8 (7, 8) sts. Working in St st, increase 1 st at each edge every other row 3 (4, 4) times—14 (15, 16) sts. Work even until the piece measures 5½ (7, 8½)"/14 (18, 21.5) cm from the beginning, ending with a WS row. Place sts on a holder.

2 **Right leg**: Work as for the left leg. Leave sts on the needle.

3 **Join legs, next row (RS)**: K 14 (15, 16) sts from the right leg, cast on 2 sts (crotch), then k 14 (15, 16) sts from the left leg—30 (32, 34) sts. Work even in St st until the piece measures 13 (14½, 16)"/33 (37, 40.5) cm from the crotch, ending with a WS row.

4 **Neck shaping, next row (RS)**: K 11 (12, 12) sts. Join a second ball of yarn and bind off the center 8 (8, 10) sts, then knit to the end. Working both sides at the same time with separate balls of yarn, bind off 2 sts from each neck edge once—9 (10, 10) sts. Place sts for each shoulder on holders for later finishing.

front

5 Work as for back through leg joining. Work 3 more rows even on 30 (32, 34) sts, ending with a WS row.

6 **Separate for button/buttonhole plackets, next row (RS)**: K 16 (17, 18) sts. Join a second ball of yarn and cast on 2 sts, then knit to the end. Work both sides at the same time with separate balls of yarn. **Next row**: Left side—p 14 (15, 16) sts, k2 (button placket); right side—k2 (buttonhole placket), p 14 (15, 16) sts. Continue as established, working the button/buttonhole placket sts in Garter st for 2"/5 cm, ending with a WS row.

7 **Buttonhole, next row (RS)**: Work the left side as established; right side—k1, yo, k2tog, k to the end. Repeat the buttonhole row every 2½ (3, 3½)"/6.5 (7.5, 9) cm, 3 more times. Work 2 rows even.

8 **Neck shaping**: Bind off from each neck edge 5 sts once, then decrease 1 st at each neck edge 2 (2, 3) times—9 (10, 10) sts. Work even until the front is the same length as the back. Leave sts on the needle.

9 Sew the bottom edge of the buttonhole placket in place over the button placket.

shoulder seams

10 With the *wrong* sides facing each other, and the front of the garment facing you, place sts of the back and front right shoulders on two parallel dpns. The seam will be visible on the RS of the garment. **Work three-needle bind off as follows**: With

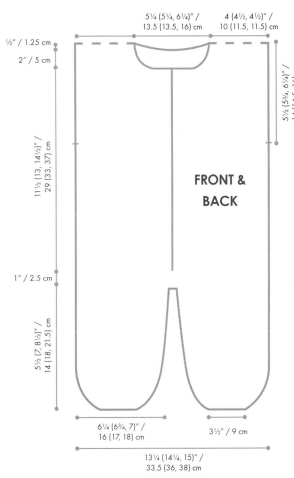

5¼ (5¼, 6¼)" / 13.5 (13.5, 16) cm

4 (4½, 4½)" / 10 (11.5, 11.5) cm

½" / 1.25 cm

2" / 5 cm

5½ (5¾, 6¼)" / 14 (14.5, 16) cm

11½ (13, 14½)" / 29 (33, 37) cm

1" / 2.5 cm

5½ (7, 8½)" / 14 (18, 21.5) cm

FRONT & BACK

6¼ (6¾, 7)" / 16 (17, 18) cm

3½" / 9 cm

13¼ (14¼, 15)" / 33.5 (36, 38) cm

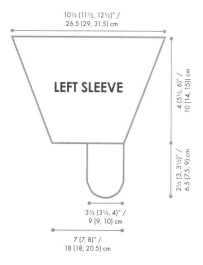

10½ (11½, 12½)" /
26.5 (29, 31.5) cm

LEFT SLEEVE

4 (5½, 6)" /
10 (14, 15)) cm

2½ (3, 3½)" /
6.5 (7.5, 9) cm

3½ (3½, 4)" /
9 (9, 10) cm

7 (7, 8)" /
18 (18, 20.5) cm

a third dpn, k the first stitch from the front needle together with the first stitch from the back needle, *k next stitch from the front and back needles together, slip first st over second st to bind off; repeat from * until all sts are bound off. Cut the yarn and pull the end through the loop. Repeat for the left side.

left sleeve

11 Place markers on the front and back 5¼ (5¾, 6¼)"/13.5 (14.5, 16) cm down from shoulder seams.

12 With the RS facing and straight needles, pick up and k 24 (26, 28) sts between the markers. Work in St st until the sleeve measures 4 (5½, 6)"/10 (14, 15) cm, ending with a WS row, and *at the same time*, decrease 1 st at each edge every fourth row 2 (3, 4) times, then every other row 2 (2, 1) times—16 (16, 18) sts.

13 Mitten flap, next row (RS): Bind off 8 (8, 9) sts, k to end. Continue on the remaining 8 (8, 9) sts for the mitten flap. Work even in St st for 1½ (2, 2½)"/4 (5, 6.5) cm, ending with a WS row. Decrease 1 st at each edge on the next and the following following RS row—4 (4, 5) sts remain. Bind off sts.

right sleeve

14 Work as for the left sleeve, working the mitten flap on the opposite side of the sleeve.

mitten covers (make 2)

15 Cast on 8 (8, 9) sts. Work in Garter st for 4 rows. Then work in St st until the piece measures 2½ (3, 3½)"/6.5 (7.5, 9) cm from the beginning, ending with a WS row. Decrease 1 st at each edge on the next and the following RS row—4 (4, 5) sts. Bind off sts.

finishing

16 Sew the side, leg, crotch, and sleeve seams. Sew the mitten covers to the ends of the mitten flaps, lapping the bottom edges of covers 1"/2.5 cm over the bound off edges of the sleeves. Sew the buttons to the button band opposite the buttonholes.

hood

17 With RS facing and straight needles, begin at the right front neck edge and pick up and k 28 (28, 30) sts evenly around the neck, including the button/buttonhole plackets. Keeping the first and last 2 sts in Garter st and the center 24 (24, 26) sts in St st, work 1 row even. **Next row (RS)**: K 9 (9, 10), place a marker, k10, place a marker, then knit to the end.

18 Work 1 row even. **Increase, next row (RS)**: [Knit to the marker, slip the marker, knit into the front and back of the next st] twice, knit to end—2 sts increased. Repeat these last 2 rows 3 times more—36 (36, 38) sts. Work even until the hood measures 8 (8½, 9)"/20.5 (21.5, 23) cm.

19 Divide sts evenly onto 2 dpns. Beginning at the front edge of the hood, work a three-needle bind off, as for the shoulder seams.

pompom

20 Wrap CC around four fingers 100 times. Remove your fingers and wrap a 12"/30.5 cm strand around the center twice. Pull snug and tie. Cut the loops and trim the ends to form a pompom. Use the 12"/30.5 cm strand of yarn to tie the pompom tightly to the top of the hood.

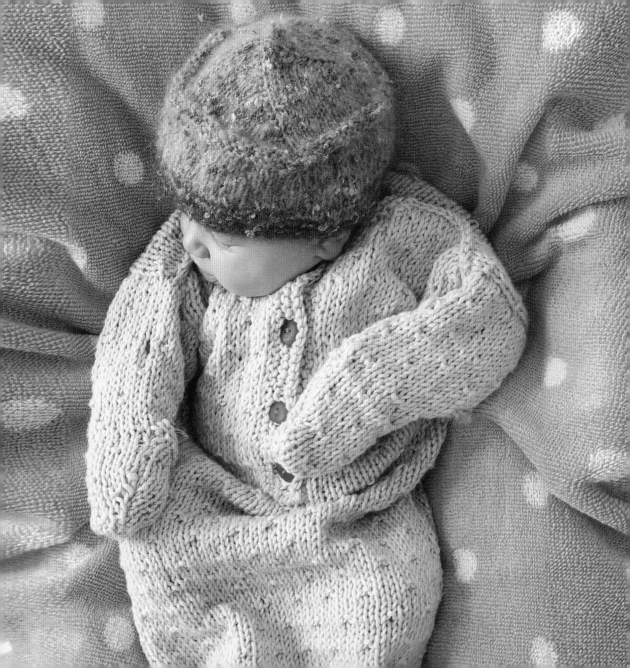

Sleepy Time

This lush sleep sac is a layette classic, the luxurious answer for baby's first sleep comfort. Light and soft, it is knit in earth-friendly bamboo yarn. The drawstring bottom keeps baby snug and happy in dreamland.

• **beginner**

sizes

Newborn (3, 6) months
Finished chest (buttoned): 19 (20½, 22)"/48 (52, 56) cm
Finished length, shoulder to hem: 20 (23, 27)"/51 (58.5, 68.5) cm

materials

Sport weight cotton or bamboo yarn for sleep sac:
405 (505, 635) yards/370 (465, 580) meters in MC; 20 yards/20 meters in CC
Multicolor mohair yarn for hat : 45 (55, 60) yards/45 (50, 55) meters in MC; 10 (15, 15) yards/10 (15, 15) meters in CC
Straight needles: Size 6 US (4 mm)
Double pointed needles (dpns), set of three: Size 6 US (4 mm)
Stitch holders and markers
Four ½"/1.25 cm buttons

gauge

20 sts and 28 rows = 4"/10 cm over pattern stitch.

✓ *Always check gauge to save time and ensure a perfect fit. Adjust needle size as necessary.*

pipsqueak profile

model: *Lydia or Lydie*

faves: *Milk, milk, and more milk*

hobby: *Squeaking*

loves: *Mommy, brother Myles, and pillow Boppy*

hates: *Being hungry or wet*

Photographed in Classic Elite Yarns Bam Boo (50g/77yds): #4920 Citrine (MC) and #4988 Melon (CC). Hat photographed in Berger du Nord Multico (50g/98yds): #5043 (MC) and #5049 (CC). Sample knit by Nita Young.

Bird's Eye Pattern

(Multiple of 4 sts plus 3)

Row 1 Knit

Row 2 Purl

Row 3 K3, * p1, k3; repeat from * to end

Rows 4 Purl

Row 5 Knit

Row 6 Purl

Row 7 K1, p1, *k3, p1; repeat from *, end k1

Row 8 Purl

Repeat rows 1-8 for pattern stitch

back

1 With straight needles and MC, cast on 47 (51, 55) sts. Work in Garter st (k every row) for 4 rows. Work rows 1-8 of Bird's Eye Pattern.

2 **Next row (RS)**: K 3 (5, 4), [yo, k2tog, k 6 (6, 7)] 5 times, yo, k2tog, k 2 (4, 4). Starting with row 2, continue in pattern until the piece measures 20 (23, 27)"/51 (58.5, 68.5) cm from the beginning, ending with a WS row. **Next row (RS)**: Work 14 (15, 17) sts and place on a holder for the back right shoulder; join a second ball of yarn and bind off 19 (21, 21) sts for the back neck; work to the end in pattern and place the remaining 14 (15, 17) sts on another holder for the back left shoulder.

front

3 Work as for the back until the piece measures 12½ (15½, 19½)"/ 31.5 (39.5, 49.5) cm from the beginning, ending with a WS row.

4 **Next row (RS)**: Work 22 (24, 26) sts; join a second ball of yarn and bind off 3 sts; work to the end of the row. Working both sides with separate balls of yarn, continue in pattern until the piece measures 18½ (21½, 25½)"/47 (54.5, 64.5) cm from the beginning.

5 **Shape neck**: Bind off 3 sts from each neck edge 1 (2, 2) times; bind off 2 sts from each neck edge 1 (0, 0) times, then decrease 1 st each neck edge 3 times—14 (15, 17) sts remain each side. Work even in pattern until the front is the same length as the back, ending with a WS row. Leave the sts on the needle.

6   Buttonbands: With RS facing, straight needles and MC, pick up and knit 30 sts along the right front edge. Work in Garter st for 2 rows. **Buttonholes, next row (WS)**: K1, yo, k2tog, [k7, yo, k2tog] 3 times. Knit 1 more row. Bind off sts. Work the left buttonband as for the right, omitting buttonholes. Lap the right buttonband over the left and sew the bottom edges in place.

shoulder seams

7   With the *wrong* sides facing each other and the front of the garment facing you, place sts of the back and front left shoulders on two parallel dpns. Shoulder seams will be visible on the RS of the garment. **Work three-needle bind off as follows**: With a third dpn, k the first st from the front needle together with the first st from the back needle, *k the next st from the front and back needles together, slip the first st over the second st to bind off; repeat from * until all sts are bound off. Cut the yarn and pull the end through the loop. Repeat for the right side.

sleeves

8   Left sleeve: Place markers on the front and back, 4¾ (4¾, 5)"/12 (12, 12.5) cm down from the shoulder seam. With RS facing, straight needles and MC, pick up and k 47 (47, 51) sts between the markers. Starting with row 2, work in Bird's Eye Pattern until the sleeve measures 4 (5, 6½)"/10 (12.5, 16.5) cm, and *at the same time*, decrease 1 st each edge every sixth row 0 (0, 3) times, then every fourth row 1 (7, 6), then every other row 10 (2, 0) times—25 (29, 33) sts, ending with a WS row.

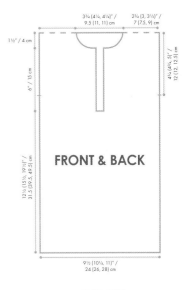

FRONT & BACK

3¾ (4¼, 4¼)" / 9.5 (11, 11) cm

2¾ (3, 3½)" / 7 (7.5, 9) cm

1½" / 4 cm

6" / 15 cm

4¾ (4¾, 5)" / 12 (12, 12.5) cm

12½ (15½, 19¼)" / 31.5 (39.5, 49.5) cm

9½ (10¼, 11)" / 24 (26, 28) cm

LEFT SLEEVE

9½ (9½, 10)" / 24 (24, 25.5) cm

4 (5, 6½)" / 10 (12.5, 16.5) cm

3 (3½, 4)" / 7.5 (9, 10) cm

2½ (2¾, 3½)" / 6.5 (7, 9) cm

5 (5¾, 6½)" / 12.5 (14.5, 16.5) cm

9 **Mitten flap, next row (RS)**: Bind off 12 (14, 16) sts, then work to end. Continue on 13 (15, 17) remaining sts and work even in pattern for 2 (2½, 2¾)"/5 (6.5, 7) cm, ending with a WS row. Decrease 1 st each edge on the next and every other row 4 (4, 5) times total. Bind off the remaining 5 (7, 7) sts.

10 **Right sleeve:** Work as for the left sleeve, working the mitten flap on the opposite side of sleeve.

mitten covers (make 2)

11 With MC, cast on 13 (15, 17) sts. Work in Garter stitch for 4 rows. Work in Stockinette st until the piece measures 2½ (3, 3¼)"/6.5 (7.5, 8) cm, from the beginning, ending with a WS row. Decrease 1 st at each edge on the next and every other row 4 (4, 5) times total. Bind off the remaining 5 sts.

finishing

12 Sew the side and sleeve seams.

13 Sew the mitten covers to the ends of the mitten flaps, lapping the bottom edges of the covers ½"/1.25 cm over the bound off edges of the sleeves.

14 Sew the buttons to the button band.

15 **Neckband**: With RS facing, straight needles and MC, begin at the right front. Pick up and k 11 sts along the right neck edge, including the button band, 19 (21, 21) sts along the back neck, and 11 sts along the left neck edge, including the button band—41 (43, 43) sts. Work in Garter st for 2 rows. Bind off sts. **I-cord drawstring**: With dpns and CC, cast on 3 sts. K3. *Do not turn the work. Slide sts to the other end of the needle to work the next row from the RS: k3; repeat from * for 20 (21½, 23)"/50.5 (54.5, 58.5) cm. Bind off sts. Weave the I-cord through the yarn overs at the bottom of the garment and tie a bow.

hat

1 With dpns and MC, cast on 4 sts. **Work I-cord as follows**: K4 sts. *Do not turn the work. Slide sts to the other end of the needle to work the next row from the RS and k4; repeat from * for 1"/2.5 cm. Increase 1 st in each st on the next row to 8 sts. Divide sts evenly on 4 dpns (2 sts on each needle). Join and work in rounds of St st (k every round), increase 1 st at end of every needle every round (therefore, 4 sts increased every round) until there are 76 (84, 92) sts, or 19 (21, 23) sts on each needle.

2 Purl 3 rounds for reverse St st ridge. Work in St st for 1¼ (1½, 1¾)"/3 (4, 4.5) cm. Change to CC and knit 1 round. Change to MC and knit 1 round. Repeat the last two rounds one more time. Place sts on a circular needle.

3 With dpns and CC, cast on 4 sts. **Work I-cord bind off as follows**: K4 sts. *Do not turn the work. Slide sts to the other end of the needle to work the next row from the RS and k3, knit the last st from the dpn together with the first st from the circular needle *through the back loops*; repeat from * until all sts from the circular needle have been worked. Bind off the remaining 4 sts. Sew the ends of the I-cord together.

Mo-Mo Kimono

two-toned mohair
kimono jacket
with i-cord ties

An outerwear take on the classic kimono, this light-weight but warm jacket is a QuickKnit with panache. Mohair is a wonderful fiber for kids' wear, as it is light but durable, cozy and warm. Classic Elite Yarns La Gran Mohair is available in an extensive array of gorgeous colors.

* **beginner quickknit**

sizes

3 months (6 months, 1, 2, 3) years
Finished chest, closed: 19 (22, 24, 26, 28)"/48 (56, 61, 66, 71) cm
Finished length: 9 (10, 12, 13, 14)"/23 (25.5, 30.5, 33, 35.5) cm

materials

Mohair yarn: 165 (205, 270, 330, 395) yards/150 (190, 250, 305, 365) meters in MC; 30 yards/30 meters in CC
Straight needles: Size 9 US (5.5 mm)
Stitch holders and markers
Double-pointed needles (dpns), set of three: Size 9 US (5.5mm)
One small button

gauge

16 sts and 24 rows = 4"/10 cm over Stockinette Stitch (St st).

✓ Always check gauge to save time and ensure a perfect fit. Adjust needle size as necessary.

pipsqueak profile

model: Jane Margaret, aka BooBah

yummies: Pancakes!

tunes: The Beatles

hobby: Spinning in the kitchen till I fall down

loves: Mom's high heels

favorite stuffie: Big Kitty

Photographed in Classic Elite Yarns La Gran (42 g/90 yds): #6519 Cameo Pink (MC) and #61532 Positively Pink (CC). Sample knit by Donna Michaud

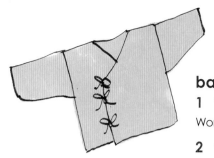

back

1 With straight needles and MC, cast on 38 (44, 48, 52, 56) sts. Work in Garter st (k every row) for 4 rows.

2 Work in St st until the piece measures 9 (10, 12, 13, 14)"/23 (25.5, 30.5, 33, 35.5) cm from the beginning, ending with a WS row.

3 **Next row (RS)**: K 12 (14, 16, 17, 19) sts and place on a holder for the back right shoulder. Bind off the next 14 (16. 16, 18, 18) sts for the back neck. K the remaining sts and place on a second holder for the back left shoulder.

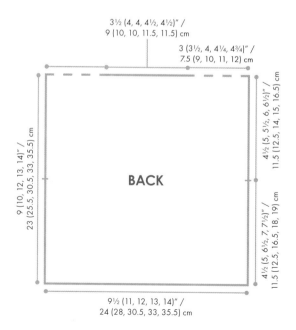

3½ (4, 4, 4½, 4½)" / 9 (10, 10, 11.5, 11.5) cm

3 (3½, 4, 4¼, 4¾)" / 7.5 (9, 10, 11, 12) cm

9 (10, 12, 13, 14)" / 23 (25.5, 30.5, 33, 35.5) cm

BACK

4½ (5, 5½, 6, 6½)" / 11.5 (12.5, 14, 15, 16.5) cm

4½ (5, 6½, 7, 7½)" / 11.5 (12.5, 16.5, 18, 19) cm

9½ (11, 12, 13, 14)" / 24 (28, 30.5, 33, 35.5) cm

left front

4 With straight needles and MC, cast on 25 (29, 31, 34, 36) sts. Work in Garter st for 4 rows.

5 **Next and all RS rows**: Knit. **All WS rows**: K3 (Garter st trim), the purl to the end. Repeat the last two rows until the piece measures 4¼ (4¾, 6¼, 6¾, 7¾)"/11 (12, 16, 17, 19.5) cm from the beginning, ending with a WS row.

6 **Buttonhole, next row (RS)**: K to the last 4 sts, k2tog, yo, k2. **Next row**: K3, then purl to the end.

7 **Shape neck, next row (RS)**: K to the last 5 sts, k2tog, k3. Repeat the last 2 rows 12 (14, 14, 16, 16) times more—12 (14, 16, 17, 19) sts. Work even, if necessary, to the same length as the back. Place sts on a holder for the front left shoulder.

right front

8 Work as for the back, reversing the Garter st edge and neck shaping and omitting the buttonhole. End with a WS row. Leave sts on the needle.

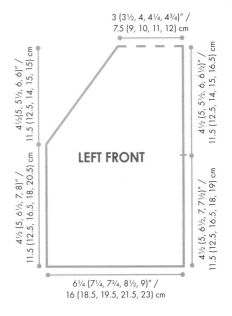

3 (3½, 4, 4¼, 4¾)" / 7.5 (9, 10, 11, 12) cm

4½ (5, 5½, 6, 6)" / 11.5 (12.5, 14, 15, 15) cm

4½ (5, 5½, 6, 6½)" / 11.5 (12.5, 14, 15, 16.5) cm

LEFT FRONT

4½ (5, 6½, 7, 8)" / 11.5 (12.5, 16.5, 18, 20.5) cm

4½ (5, 6½, 7, 7½)" / 11.5 (12.5, 16.5, 18, 19) cm

6¼ (7¼, 7¾, 8½, 9)" / 16 (18.5, 19.5, 21.5, 23) cm

shoulder seams

9 With *wrong* sides facing each other, and the front of the sweater facing you, place sts from the back and front right shoulders on two parallel dpns. The seam will be visible on the RS of the sweater. **Work a three-needle bind off as follows:** With a third dpn, k the first stitch from the front needle together with the first stitch from the back needle, *k the next stitch from the front and back needles together, slip the first st over the second st to bind off; repeat from * until all sts are bound off. Cut the yarn and pull the end through the loop. Repeat for the left side.

sleeves

10 Place markers on front and back, 4½ (5, 5½, 6, 6½)"/11.5 (12.5, 14, 15, 16.5) cm down from shoulder seams.

11 With RS facing, straight needles and MC, pick up and k 36 (40, 44, 48, 52) sts between the markers for the sleeves.

12 Working in St st, decrease 1 st each edge every sixth row 0 (0, 0, 1, 2) times, then every fourth row 6 (8, 9, 10, 10) times—

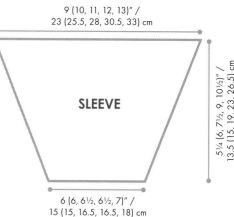

9 (10, 11, 12, 13)" /
23 (25.5, 28, 30.5, 33) cm

5¼ (6, 7½, 9, 10½)" /
13.5 (15, 19, 23, 26.5) cm

SLEEVE

6 (6, 6½, 6½, 7)" /
15 (15, 16.5, 16.5, 18) cm

24 (24, 26, 26, 28) sts. Work even, if necessary, until the sleeve measures 4½ (5¾, 6¾, 8¼, 9¾)"/ 11.5 (14.5, 17, 21, 24.5) cm, ending with a RS row.

13 Work 4 rows in Garter st. Bind off sts loosely and evenly.

finishing

14 Sew the sleeve and side seems. Overlap the right front over the left so that the fronts lie flat. Sew a button to the inside of the right front to correspond to the buttonhole on the left front.

I-cord ties (make 6)

15 With dpns and CC, cast on 3 sts. K3. *Do not turn the work. Slide sts to the other end of the needle to work the next row from the RS and k3; repeat from * for 5"/12.5 cm. Bind off sts.

16 Sew 3 ties to the right front edge: the first one at 1"/2.5 cm from bottom, the second one just below the beginning of the neck shaping, and the third one centered between the other two. Sew the remaining 3 ties to the left front so that the ties line up. Knot and tie into bows to close.

Darling!

short and sassy jumper
with faux cabled
bodice and matching
diaper cover

Lovely on warmer days as is, this jumper is still cute over a blouse for colder climes. This faux cable adds a dressy detail to this little charmer, and couldn't be easier to knit.

● ● ● **intermediate beginner**

sizes
3-6 months (6-12 months, 12-18 months)
Dress finished chest: 16 (18, 20)"/40.5 (45.5, 51) cm
Dress finished length: 12 (14½, 16)"/30.5 (37, 40.5) cm
Diaper cover finished waist (buttoned): 14½ (16, 17)"/37 (40.5, 43) cm
Diaper cover length (unbuttoned): 14 (15, 16)"/35.5 (38, 40.5) cm

materials
Worsted weight yarn: 345 (450, 525) yards/315 (415, 480) meters for dress; 185 (215, 245) yards/170 (200, 225) meters for diaper cover
Straight needles: Size 8 US (5mm)
Circular needles, 16"/40.5 cm and 40"/101.5 cm: Size 8 US (5mm)
Stitch holders and markers
Eight ½"/2 cm buttons
One yard ½"/2 cm elastic

gauges
18 sts and 24 rows = 4"/10cm over Stockinette st (St st)
24 sts and 26 rows = 4" over pattern stitch.

✓ *Always check gauge to save time and ensure a perfect fit. Adjust needle size as necessary.*

pipsqueak profile

model: *Anna, or Anna-Banana to my friends*

yummies: *Milk—and bananas, of course!*

hobby: *Poking Mom in the face*

loves: *Eating*

hates: *Having my face wiped*

tunes: *Hip-hop*

Photographed in Jil Eaton MinnowMerino (50g/77yds): #4788 Tangerine. Sample knit by Donna Michaud

Mock Cable

(Multiple of 4 sts plus 2)

Right twist (RT) K2tog leaving both sts on needle; insert RH needle between 2 sts, and k first st again; then slip both sts from needle

Row 1 P2 *k2, p2; repeat from * to end

Rows 2 and 4 K2, *p2, k2; repeat from * to end

Row 3 P2, *RT, p2; repeat from * to end

Repeat rows 1-4 for pattern stitch

dress skirt

1 With the larger circular needle, cast on 200 (216, 232) sts. Do not join sts. Work back and forth as follows: Starting with a knit row, work 7 rows in St st. K the next row on the WS for the turning ridge for the hem. K the next row on the RS and join sts. Place a marker.

2 Begin working in rounds. Work in St st (k every round) until the piece measures 7½ (9½, 10½)"/19 (24, 26.5) cm from the turning ridge.

3 **Next round:** K2tog around—100 (108, 116) sts, changing to a shorter circular needle, if necessary.

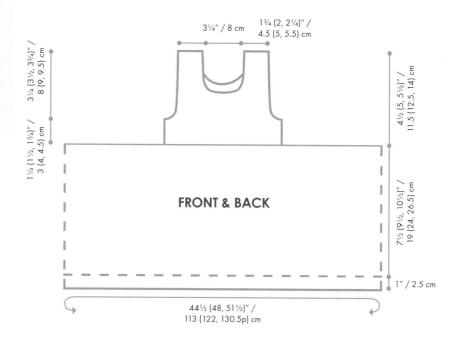

3¼" / 8 cm

1¾ (2, 2¼)" / 4.5 (5, 5.5) cm

3¼ (3½, 3¾)" / 8 (9, 9.5) cm

1¼ (1½, 1¾)" / 3 (4, 4.5) cm

4½ (5, 5½)" / 11.5 (12.5, 14) cm

FRONT & BACK

7½ (9½, 10½)" / 19 (24, 26.5) cm

1" / 2.5 cm

44½ (48, 51½)" / 113 (122, 130.5p) cm

dress bodice

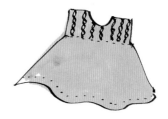

4 Divide for front and back: With straight needles, k 50 (54, 58) sts for the front. Place the remaining sts on a holder for the back.

5 Bodice front: Working back and forth on the front sts only, work in the Mock Cable pattern for 1¼ (1½, 1¾)"/3 (4, 4.5) cm.

6 Armhole shaping: Continue to work back and forth in pattern, binding off 2 sts at the beginning of the next 2 rows, then decrease 1 st each side every other row 3 times—40 (44, 48) sts. Work even until the bodice measures 2½ (3, 3½)"/6.5 (7.5, 9) cm, ending with a WS row.

7 Neck shaping, next row (RS): Work 15 (16, 18) sts. Join a second ball of yarn and bind off the center 10 (12, 12) sts for the neck. Work to the end. Working both sides at the same time with separate balls of yarn, bind off 2 sts from each neck edge twice, then decrease 1 st from each neck edge 1 (0, 0) time—10 (12, 14) sts remain on each side. Work even until the bodice measures 4½ (5, 5½)"/11.5 (12.5, 14) cm, ending with a WS row.

8 Buttonholes, next row (RS): Work both sides as follows: Work 2 (3, 3) sts, yo, k2tog, work 3 sts, yo, k2tog, then work to the end. Work 3 more rows in pattern. Bind off both sides in pattern.

9 Bodice back: Using sts from the back holder, work as for the front until the bodice measures 3 (3½, 4)"/7.5 (9, 10) cm. Work the neck shaping as for the front. Continue even until the back is the same length as the front, omitting buttonholes. Bind off both sides in pattern.

finishing dress

10 Sew the seam in the hem. Turn the hem to the WS along the turning ridge and sew in place.

11 Sew buttons to the back shoulders, opposite the buttonholes.

diaper cover

1 With straight needles, cast on 38 (42, 46) sts. Work in Mock Cable pattern for 3 (3½, 4)" /7.5 (9, 10) cm. Place markers at the side edges.

2 Increase 1 st each side every seventh (seventh, tenth) row 3 (3, 2) times—44 (48, 50) sts. Work even until the piece measures 10 (11, 12)"/25.5 (28, 30.5) cm from the beginning. Place markers at the side edges.

3 Increase 1 st each side every RS row 3 times. Cast on 4 sts at the beginning of the next 4 rows, and 8 (10, 12) sts at the beginning of the next 2 rows—82 (90, 96) sts. Work even until the piece measures 13 (14, 15)"/33 (35.5, 38) cm from the beginning, ending with a WS row.

4 Buttonholes, next row (RS): Work 2 sts, yo, k2tog, k1, yo, k2tog, work to the last 7 sts, k2tog, yo, k1, k2tog, yo, then work to the end. Work even until the piece measures 14 (15, 16)"/35.5 (38, 40.5) cm from the beginning. Bind off in pattern.

finishing diaper cover

5 **Leg casing**: With RS facing, pick up and k 42 (45, 48) sts evenly between the markers. Knit 1 row. **Next row (RS)**: K. Continue in St st for 1"/2.5 cm. Bind off sts.

6 Fold the casing to the WS and sew in place, leaving an opening at each end for elastic. Thread the elastic through the casing and adjust to fit. Secure the elastic and sew the openings closed.

7 Sew buttons to the RS of the front flap opposite the buttonholes. The ends of the tabs should be separated by 1"/2.5 cm when wrapped around the front flap.

Jack Be Nimble

This light-as-a-feather Elfin hat and matching booties will brighten those winter days, keeping Baby toasty and warm. Quickly knit, with a curly mohair trim.

• • • **intermediate/advanced beginner**

hat sizes

3 (6, 12, 18) months
Finished circumference: 14¼ (16, 18, 19½)"/36 (40.5, 45.5, 50) cm

bootie sizes

3 (6, 12) months
Foot circumference: 5¼ (5¼, 6¼)"/13.5 (13.5, 16) cm
Foot length: 3½ (4, 4½)"/9 (10, 11.5) cm

materials

Worsted weight yarn: 60 (70, 80, 85) yards/55 (65, 75, 80) meters in MC; 25 (30, 35, 40) yards/25 (30, 35, 40) meters in A for hat; 50 (50, 65) yards/45 (45, 60) in MC; 10 yards/10 meters in A for booties
Mohair yarn for trim (B): 50 (60, 70, 70) yards/45 (55, 65, 65) meters for hat; 25 (25, 30) yards/25 (25, 30) meters for booties
Double-pointed needles (dpns), set of 5: Size 7 US (4.5mm)
16"/40.5 cm circular needle: Size 7 US (4.5mm)

gauge

18 sts and 26 rows = 4"/10 cm in Stockinette st (St st) using size MC

✓ *Always check gauge to save time and ensure a perfect fit.*
Adjust needle size as necessary.

elfin hat and matching booties

pipsqueak profile

model: *Gabriel, nickname Boo-Boo*

yummies: *Lasagna*

tunes: *Theme music for Law and Order*

hobby: *Throwing things into the toilet, especially my pacifiers, Mommy's keys, and—if I can find it—Mommy's phone*

loves: *Climbing up and down stairs*

hates: *Not being allowed in the bathroom*

Photographed in Jil Eaton MinnowMerino (50g/77yds): #4735 Chartreuse (MC), #4720 Aqua Aqua (A) and Classic Elite Yarns La Gran Mohair (42g/90yds): #6567 Aqua Tint (B). Sample knit by Stephanie Doben.

Fringe Loop Stitch

*K into front of st, yf between the needles, loop yarn around your thumb, yb, k into back of same st, being careful not to pull out loop; slip both newly-created sts to LH needle, k2tog—1 Fringe Loop St made; repeat from * across.

hat

1 With dpns and MC, cast on 4 sts. Knit into the front and back of each st (k1f&b) across—8 sts. Divide sts onto 4 needles, with 2 sts on each needle. Join sts in a round, being careful not to twist sts. K 1 round even. **Next round**: *K to last st on needle, k1f&b; repeat from * around—4 sts increased. Repeat the last 2 rounds until there are 16 (18, 20, 22) sts on each needle—64 (72, 80, 88) sts total.

2 Change to a circular needle, if desired. Work even in St st (k each round) for 1½ (2, 2½, 3)"/4 (5, 6.5, 7.5) cm *more*. Cut the yarn.

3 Change to A and k 8 rounds. Cut the yarn.

4 Change to B and k 3 rounds.

5 **Next round**: Work 2 Fringe Loop sts. Pass the first st on the RH needle over the second st to bind off 1 st. Continue working Fringe Loop st and binding off. Pull the yarn through the last st to fasten off.

tassel

6 Wrap B around four fingers 50 times. Remove your fingers and pull through the 8"/20.5 cm strand of yarn. Tie. Wrap another strand twice around, 1"/2.5 cm down from the top. Tie. Cut the loops at the other end and trim evenly. Use the 8"/20.5 cm strand to tie the tassel tightly to the top of the hat.

booties

1 **Cuff**: With dpns and B, cast on 24 (24, 28) sts. Divide sts evenly onto 3 needles. Join in a round, being careful not to twist sts. **Round 1**: Work Fringe Loop St around. Knit 2 rounds even. Cut the yarn.

2 Change to A and k 8 rounds. Cut the yarn.

3 Change to MC and work in k1, p1 rib for 1½"/4 cm.

4 **Divide for heel, next round**: K 6 (6, 7) sts from the first needle for the heel. Without working, slip the next 12 (12, 14) sts on two needles for the instep. Slip the last 6 (6, 7) sts onto the first needle for the heel—12 (12, 14) sts total on the first needle for the heel.

5 Working back and forth on 12 (12, 14) heel sts, begin with a WS (purl) row and work in St st, slipping the first stitch of each row, for a ¾ (1, 1)"/2 (2.5, 2.5) cm for heel flap. End with a RS row.

6 **Turn heel, next row (WS)**: Slip 1, p6, p2tog, p1, turn. **Next row**: Slip 1, k 3 (3, 1), ssk, k1, turn. **Next row**: Slip 1, p 4 (4, 2), p2tog, p1, turn. **Next row**: Slip 1, k 5 (5, 3), ssk, k1.

7 **Size 12 months only**: Turn. **Next row**: Slip 1, p4, p2tog, p1, turn. **Next row**: Slip 1, k5, ssk, k1.

8 **All sizes**: 8 sts remain on needle 1.

9 **Instep**: Begin working in rounds again. With RS facing, pick up and k 5 (6, 6) sts along the right edge of the heel flap with needle 1; k 12 (12, 14) sts from the instep with needle 2; pick up and k 5 (6, 6) sts along the left edge of the heel flap with needle 3 and then knit the first 4 sts from needle 1—30 (32, 34) sts total; 9 (10, 10) sts on needles 1 and 3, 12 (12, 14) sts on needle 2.

10 Rounds begin at the center of the heel. Work 1 round even. **Next round**: Needle 1—k to last 3 sts, k2tog, k1; Needle 2—k across; Needle 3—k1, ssk, k to end—2 sts decreased. Repeat the last 2 rounds until 24 (24, 28) sts remain. Work even in St st until the foot measures 2¼ (2¾, 3)"/5.5 (7, 7.5) cm from the back of the heel, *or 1¼ (1¼, 1½)"/3 (3, 4) cm less than the total desired length.*

11 **Shape toe, next (decrease) round**: Needle 1—k to last 3 sts on needle, k2tog, k1; Needle 2—k1, ssk, k to last 3 sts, k2tog, k1; Needle 3—k1, ssk, k to end. Work 1 round even. Repeat decrease round next and every other round until 4 sts rem. Cut the yarn and pull through sts to fasten off.

Jester

A fair-isle that looks more difficult than it is, as you only work with two colors at a time. Gloriously multicolored in eight different hues, this cotton pull is a delectable treat.

• • • **intermediate**

sizes

6 months (1, 2, 3) years
Finished chest: 21½ (24, 26½, 29)"/55 (61, 67, 73.5) cm
Finished length: 10 (12, 13, 14)"/25.5 (30.5, 33, 35.5) cm

materials

DK weight cotton: 70 (90, 110, 135) yards/65 (85, 100, 125) meters in D; 55 (70, 85, 105) yards/50 (65, 80, 100) meters in A and B; 40 (50, 60, 75) yards/40 (45, 55, 70) meters in C and D; 30 (40, 50, 60) yards/30 (40, 45, 55) meters in F, G, and H
Straight needles: Sizes 6 and 7 US (4 and 4.5mm)
Stitch holders and markers
Four ¾"/2 cm buttons

gauge

20 sts and 25 rows = 4"/10 cm over St st and chart pattern using larger needles.

 Always check gauge to save time and ensure a perfect fit. Adjust needle size as necessary.

a multi-colored fair-isle delight!

pipsqueak profile

model: Lucas, or Bubba for short

yummies: I'm an avocado baby!

tunes: Reggae

hobby: Whistling all day long

loves: Animals, books, playing outside

hates: Wearing a bib

Photographed in Rowan Handknit Cotton (50g/93yds): #305 Lupin/Lavender (A), #287 Diana/Blue (B), #219 Gooseberry/Lt. Green (C), #318 Seafarer/Aqua (D), #314 Decadent/Purple (E), #336 Sunflower/Yellow (F), #337 Tangerine Dream/Orange (G) and #215 Rosso/Red (H). Sample knit by Joan Cassidy. **For the puppy sweater, see *PuppyKnits* by Jil Eaton.**

back

1   With smaller needles and D, cast on 53 (59, 65, 71) sts. Work in k1, p1 rib for 1"/2.5cm. Increase 1 st in last (WS) row to 54 (60, 66, 72) sts.

2   Change to larger needles. Work chart pattern in St st as follows: Work the last 3 (0, 3, 0) sts of the chart, work 12-st repeat of the chart 4 (5, 5, 6) times, the work first 3 (0, 3, 0) sts of the chart. Continue in pattern as established until the piece measures 10 (12, 13, 14)"/25.5 (30.5, 33, 35.5) cm from the beginning, ending with a WS row.

Next row (RS): Work 16 (18, 20, 22) sts, bind off the next 22 (24, 26, 28) sts for the neck, then work to the end. Cut the yarns. Change to D.

3   Working both sides at the same time with separate balls of yarn, continue in St st and D on the remaining sts for 1"/2.5 cm for the button plackets. Bind off sts.

front

4   Work the same as the back until the piece measures 8 (10, 11, 12)"/20.5 (25.5, 28, 30.5) cm from the beginning, ending with a WS row.

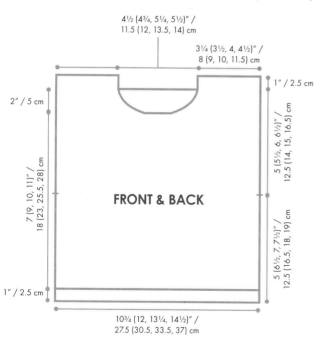

4½ (4¾, 5¼, 5½)" / 11.5 (12, 13.5, 14) cm

3¼ (3½, 4, 4½)" / 8 (9, 10, 11.5) cm

1" / 2.5 cm

2" / 5 cm

5 (5½, 6, 6½)" / 12.5 (14, 15, 16.5) cm

7 (9, 10, 11)" / 18 (23, 25.5, 28) cm

FRONT & BACK

5 (6½, 7, 7½)" / 12.5 (16.5, 18, 19) cm

1" / 2.5 cm

10¾ (12, 13¼, 14½)" / 27.5 (30.5, 33.5, 37) cm

Color Key

Lavender (A)   Purple (E)

Blue (B)   Yellow (F)

Lt green (C)   Orange (G)

Aqua (D)   Red (H)

5 Shape neck, next row (RS): Work 21 (23, 26, 28) sts in pattern. Attach a second ball of yarn as per chart and bind off the center 12 (14, 14, 16) sts for the front neck. Work to the end. Working both sides at the same time with separate balls of yarn, continue in St st and chart pattern and bind off from each neck edge 3 sts once, then decrease 1 st each neck edge every RS row 2 (2, 3, 3) times. Work even on the remaining 16 (18, 20, 22) each side until the piece measures 9¾ (11¾, 12¾, 13¾)"/25 (30, 32.5, 35) cm from the beginning, ending with a WS.

6 Buttonholes, next row (RS): Left shoulder—K 9 (11, 13, 15), yo, k2tog, k5; Right shoulder—K5, k2tog, yo, k 9 (11, 13, 15). Continue in St st and chart pattern until the piece measures 10 (12, 13, 14)"/25.5 (30.5, 33, 35.5) cm from the beginning, ending with a WS row. Bind off sts.

7 Sew two buttons to the button plackets opposite the buttonholes.

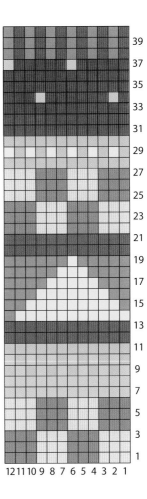

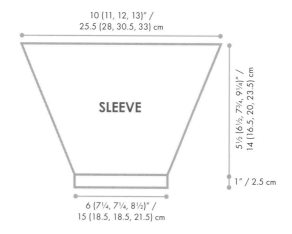

sleeves

8   With smaller needles and D, cast on 29 (33, 33, 39) sts. Work in k1, p1 rib for 1"/2.5 cm. Increase 1 (3, 3, 3) sts evenly across the last (WS) row to 30 (36, 36, 42) sts.

9   Change to larger needles. Work the chart pattern in St st as follows: Work the last 3 (0, 0, 3) sts of the chart, work 12-st repeat of the chart 2 (3, 3, 3) times, work the first 3 (0, 0, 3) sts of chart, and *at the same time*, increase 1 st each edge every sixth row 0 (0, 0, 3) times, then every fourth row 5 (8, 10, 9) times, then every other row 5 (2, 2, 0) times, working increases into the chart pattern—50 (56, 60, 66) sts. Work even until the sleeve measures 6½ (7½, 8¾, 10¼)"/16.5 (19, 22, 26) cm, *or the desired length*, from the beginning. Bind off sts.

10 (11, 12, 13)" /
25.5 (28, 30.5, 33) cm

SLEEVE

5½ (6½, 7¾, 9¼)" /
14 (16.5, 20, 23.5) cm

1" / 2.5 cm

6 (7¼, 7¼, 8½)" /
15 (18.5, 18.5, 21.5) cm

finishing

10 Sew the shoulder seams, starting from the outer edges and ending halfway to buttonholes, allowing the bound off edges to show.

11 Place markers 5 (5½, 6, 6½)"/12.5 (14, 15, 16.5) cm down from the shoulder seams on the front and back. Sew the sleeves between the markers. Sew the side and sleeve seams.

neckbands

12 **Back**: With the RS facing, smaller needles and D, begin at the right back neck edge and pick up and k 31 (33, 35, 37) sts evenly across back neck, including the sides of the button plackets. Work in k1, p1 rib for 3 rows. Bind off loosely and evenly in rib.

13 **Front**: With the RS facing, smaller needles and D, begin at the left front neck edge and pick up and k 31 (33, 35, 37) sts evenly across front neck. Work 1 row in k1, p1 rib. **Buttonhole, next row (RS)**: Rib 3, yo, k2tog, rib to last 5 sts, k2tog, yo, rib 3. Work 1 more row of ribbing. Bind off loosely and evenly in rib.

14 Sew two buttons to the back neckband.

Parfait

Luxurious, warm and cozy, the perfect combo for those chilly winter outings. Knit in luxurious cashmere, these fetching hat and mitts will be perfect for heirloom hand-me-downs, and will be a dream to knit

adorable folded hat
with drawstring and
matching mittens

- **beginner quickknit**

sizes

6-12 months (12-18 months, 18-24 months)
Hat, finished circumference: 17 (18, 19)"/43 (45.5, 48) cm
Mittens, finished length: 4 (5, 6)"/10 (12.5, 15) cm

materials

Worsted weight cashmere yarn: 140 (170, 200) yards/130 (155, 185) meters in MC; 75 (90, 105) yards/70 (85, 100) meters in CC for hat; 35 (45, 50) yards/35 (45, 50) meters in MC; 20 (25, 30) yards/20 (25, 30) meters in CC for mittens
Straight needles: size 8 US (5 mm)
Crochet hook: size H-8 (5 mm)
Stitch holders

gauge

18 sts and 27 rows = 4"/10 cm over pattern stitch

✓ *Always check gauge to save time and ensure a perfect fit. Adjust needle size as necessary.*

pip**squea**k
profile

model: *Helena*

yummies: *Scrambled eggs*

loves: *Twirling*

hates: *Diaper changes*

favorite word: *Socks*

Photographed in Classic Elite Yarns Lavish Cashmere (50 g/125 yds): #92560 Sky (MC) and #10219 Bright Pink (CC). Sample knit by Patti Waters.

Garter Ridge Pattern

Rows 1 and 3 Knit with MC
Rows 2 and 4 Purl with MC
Rows 5 and 6 Knit with CC

Repeat these 6 rows
for pattern stitch

hat

1 With MC, cast on 76 (80, 85) sts. Knit 2 rows. Starting with a knit row, work in St st until the piece measures 1"/2.5 cm, ending with a WS row.

2 Work in Garter Ridge pattern until the piece measures 7 (8, 8¾)"/18 (20.5, 22) cm from the beginning, ending with row 6 of the pattern.

3 Work in St st, with MC only, for 7 (8, 8¾)"/18 (20.5, 22) cm more—total length is 14 (16, 17½)"/35.5 (40.5, 44.5) cm. Bind off sts.

tie

4 With a crochet hook and CC, chain approximately 18"/45.5 cm. Fasten off.

finishing

5 Sew the back seam to form a tube. Fold the tube in half lengthwise, with the WS together and the RS of Garter Ridge pattern section on the outside. The fold will become the bottom edge of the hat. Gather the top of the hat and weave the tie through both layers of fabric, 1"/2.5 cm down from top. Tie a bow.

pompoms (make 2)

6 Wrap CC around four fingers 100 times. Remove your fingers and wrap 12"/30.5 cm strand of yarn around the center twice. Pull snug and tie. Cut the loops and trim the ends to form a pompom. Sew one to each end of a tie.

mittens (make 2)

1 With MC, cast on 22 (26, 30) sts. Knit 2 rows. Starting with a knit row, work in St st until the piece measures 1"/2.5 cm. Next, work in Garter Ridge pattern for 1"/2.5 cm, ending with a WS row.

2 **Thumb shaping, sizes 12-18 and 18-24 months only, next row (RS)**: Continue in pattern and work (11, 13) sts, k1f&b into the next 4 sts, work (11, 13) sts—(30, 34) sts. Work 3 rows even.

3 **Next row (RS)**: Work (13, 15) sts, k1f&b into the next 4 sts, work (13, 15) sts—(34, 38) sts. Work (13, 15) sts and place on a holder. Work 8 thumb sts, then work the remaining (13, 15) sts and place on another holder. Cut the yarn.

4 **Thumb, next row (RS)**: Working in pattern stitch, on thumb sts only, rejoin the yarn and increase 1 st each edge—10 sts. Continue in pattern until the thumb measures (1¼, 1¾)"/(3, 4.5) cm, ending with a WS row.

5 Continue with MC only. **Next row**: K2tog across. **Next row**: P2tog twice, p1. Cut the yarn and pull through remaining 5 sts. Sew the thumb seam.

6 With RS facing and keeping to pattern, work sts from the holder, pick up 4 sts across the thumb, then work sts from the other holder—(30, 34) sts.

7 **Hand, all sizes**: Work in pattern until the mitten measures 3¾ (4¾, 5¾)"/9.5 (12, 14.5) cm from the beginning, ending with a WS row.

8 Continue with MC only. **Next row**: K2tog across. **Next row**: P2tog across, end p1. **Next row**: K2tog across, k 0 (0, 1). **Next row**: P2tog across, p 1 (0, 1). Cut the yarn and pull through the remaining 2 (2, 3) sts. Sew the side seam.

ties (make 2)

9 With a crochet hook and A, chain approximately 15"/25.5 cm. Fasten off. Weave the tie through the cuff at 1"/2.5 cm from the bottom. Tie a bow.

Chanel Cardi

classic cardigan with
basket weave stitch
and wide back belt

*Worsted weight, perfect for a day in the country or
a city shopping spree, chic and charming for sure.
The basket weave pattern adds design detail, and
is a cinch to knit. The resulting fabric has a lovely
hand, and makes for a perfect fit.*

- **beginner quickknit**

sizes

3-6 months (1, 3) years
Finished chest (buttoned): 20 (24, 28)"/51 (61, 71) cm
Finished length: 9½ (12, 14½)"/24 (30.5, 37) cm

materials

Worsted weight yarn: 345 (505, 695) yards/315 (465, 635) meters
Straight needles: Size 8 US (5 mm)
Stitch holders and markers
Double-pointed needles(dpns), set of three: Size 8 US (5 mm)
Crochet hook: Size H-8 (5 mm)
Four ¾"/2 cm buttons
Two 1¼"/3 cm buttons

gauge

20 sts and 30 rows = 4"/10 cm over pattern stitch

✓ *Always check gauge to save time and ensure a perfect fit. Adjust
needle size as necessary.*

pipsqueak profile

model: *Hudson, but call
me Sunny!*

yummies: *Apples*

tunes: *Bob Marley*

hobby: *Talking on the
telephone*

loves: *Belly kisses*

hates: *Peas*

*Photographed in Jil Eaton
MinnowMerino (50g/77yds):
#4795 Violette. Sample knit by
Pam Tessier*

Basket Weave Pattern

(Multiple of 10 sts)

Rows 1, 3 and 5 *(K1, p1) twice, k6; repeat from * to end

Rows 2, 4 and 6 *K5, (p1, k1) twice, p1; repeat from * to end

Rows 7, 9 and 11 *K6, (p1, k1) twice; repeat from * to end

Rows 8, 10 and 12 *(P1, k1) twice, p1, k5; repeat from * to end

Repeat rows 1-12 for pattern stitch

back

1 With straight needles, cast on 50 (60, 70) sts. Work in Basket Weave pattern until the piece measures approximately 9½ (12, 14½)"/24 (30.5, 37) cm from the beginning, ending with row 11 (5, 11).

2 **Next row (WS)**: Work 15 (19, 23) sts and place them on a holder for the left shoulder. Bind off the next 20 (22, 24) sts for the back neck, then work the remaining sts and place them on a second holder for the right shoulder.

left front

3 With straight needles, cast on 28 (33, 38) sts. **Rows 1, 3 and 5**: K 0 (5, 0), work the next 20 (20, 30) sts in Basket Weave pattern, [k1, p1] twice, k4. **Rows 2, 4 and 6**: K3, [p1, k1] twice, p1, work the next 20 (20, 30) sts in Basket Weave pattern, k 0 (5, 0). **Rows 7, 9 and 11**: [K1, p1] 0 (2, 0) times, k 0 (1, 0), work the next 20 (20, 30) sts in Basket Weave pattern, k6, p1, k1. **Rows 8, 10 and 12**: P1, k1, p1, k5, work the next 20 (20, 30) sts in Basket Weave pattern, [p1, k1] 0 (2, 0) times, p 0 (1, 0). Work in pattern as established until the piece measures 8 (10½, 13)"/20.5 (26.5, 33) cm, ending with a RS row.

4 **Shape neck, next row (WS)**: Bind off 5 (4, 5) sts (neck edge), then work to the end in pattern. Continue to bind off from the neck edge 3 sts twice, then 2 sts 1 (2, 2) times—15 (19, 23) sts. Work even until the piece measures the same length as the back, ending with a WS row. Place sts on a holder.

5 Place markers for 4 buttons, the first ½"/1.25 cm below the neck edge, the last ½"/1.25 cm from the bottom edge, and the others spaced evenly between.

right front

6 With straight needles, cast on 28 (33, 38) sts. **Rows 1, 3 and 5**: K3, work the next 20 (20, 30) sts in Basket Weave pattern, [k1, p1] twice, k1 (6, 1). **Rows 2, 4 and 6**: K 0 (5, 0), [p1, k1] twice, p1, work the next 20 (20, 30) sts in Basket Weave pattern, k3. **Rows 7, 9 and 11**: K1, p1, k1, work the next 20 (20, 30) sts in Basket Weave pattern, k 5 (6, 5), [p1, k1] 0 (2, 0) times. **Rows 8, 10 and 12**: [P1, k1] 0 (2, 0) times, p 0 (1, 0), k5, work the next 20 (20, 30) sts in Basket Weave pattern, p1, k1, p1. Work in pattern as established to correspond to the left front, reversing the neck edge, and *at the same time*, work buttonholes opposite the markers as follows. **Buttonhole row (RS)**: Work 2 sts, yo, k2tog, work to the end.

shoulder seams

7 With *wrong* sides facing each other, and the front of the sweater facing you, place sts of the back and front right shoulders on two parallel dpns. The shoulder seam will be visible on the RS of the sweater. **Work three-needle bind off as follows**: With a third dpn, k the first stitch from the front needle together with the first stitch from the back needle, *k the next stitch from the front and back needles together, slip the first st over the second st to bind off; repeat from * until all sts are bound off. Cut the yarn and pull the end through the loop. Repeat for the left side.

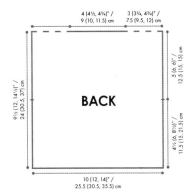

4 (4½, 4¾)" /
9 (10, 11.5) cm   3 (3¾, 4¾)" /
7.5 (9.5, 12) cm

9½ (12, 14½)" /
24 (30.5, 37) cm

5 (6, 6)" /
12.5 (15, 15) cm

BACK

4½ (6, 8½)" /
11.5 (15, 21.5) cm

10 (12, 14)" /
25.5 (30.5, 35.5) cm

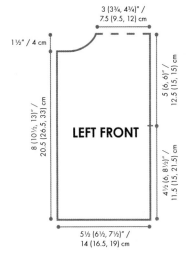

3 (3¾, 4¾)" /
7.5 (9.5, 12) cm

1½" / 4 cm

8 (10½, 13)" /
20.5 (26.5, 33) cm

5 (6, 6)" /
12.5 (15, 15) cm

LEFT FRONT

4½ (6, 8½)" /
11.5 (15, 21.5) cm

5½ (6½, 7½)" /
14 (16.5, 19) cm

sleeves

8 Place markers on the front and back, 5 (6, 6)"/12.5 (15, 15) cm down from the shoulder seams. With RS facing and straight needles, pick up and k 50 (60, 60) sts between the markers for the sleeves. Beginning with row 2, work in pattern st until the sleeve measures 6 (7½, 10½)"/15 (19, 26.5) cm, *or desired length*, ending with a WS row, and *at the same time* decrease 1 st each edge every sixth row 1 (0, 12) times, then every fourth row 9 (13, 0) times—30 (34, 36) sts. Bind off loosely and evenly.

finishing

9 Sew the sleeve and side seams. Sew four ¾"/2 cm buttons to the left front opposite the buttonholes.

10 With RS facing and a crochet hook, work 1 row of single crochet around the neck edge.

waistband

11 With straight needles, cast on 80 (95, 110) sts. Work rows 1 through 12 of Basket Weave pattern twice as follows. **All RS rows**: Work 10-st repeat of Basket Weave pattern 8 (9, 11) times, then work the first 5 sts of Basket Weave pattern 0 (1, 0) times; **All WS rows**: Work the last 5 sts of Basket Weave pattern 0 (1, 0) times, then work 10-st repeat of Basket Weave pattern 8 (9, 11) times. Bind off sts.

12 Align the center of the waistband with the center of the back halfway between the bottom edge of the sweater and the bottom of the sleeves. Tack in place at the center back. Attach one 1¼"/3 cm button at each end, sewing through the waistband and fronts. Center the buttons vertically and ½"/1.25 cm in from ends of the waistband, and align the ends of waistband with the centers of left and right fronts.

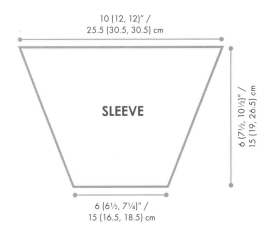

10 (12, 12)" / 25.5 (30.5, 30.5) cm

SLEEVE

6 (7½, 10½)" / 15 (19, 26.5) cm

6 (6½, 7¼)" / 15 (16.5, 18.5) cm

Models and Merci!

Writing a book such as this is quite like having a baby—months of effort spent designing, writting technical patterns, knitting, propping, photography, even the final push at the end. I am ever grateful for the boundless talents and energy from everyone involved. Nina Fuller takes all the magical photography, and you can imagine how difficult photographing babies and toddlers can be . . . Stephanie Doben is the ever-brilliant technical genius who writes and edits the patterns . . . and Anne Knudsen is my esteemed and talented editor and publisher. Thank you, thank you, thank you everyone!

about jil

Educated in art at Skidmore College, Colby College, and the Graduate School of Design at Harvard University, Jil Eaton's career as a painter and graphic designer finally succumbed to her early fashion instincts. She designs, publishes and distributes internationally an independent line of hand-knitting patterns under the MINNOWKNITS© label, and has an eponymous yarn line, Jil Eaton MinnowMerino™, a super fine washable merino wool with a micron count almost as fine as cashmere. Jil Eaton's designs have a comfortable, chic silhouette, melding the traditional with the new, adapting everything in easy-to-

knit projects with great attention to detail, fresh styling and unusual color-ways. Jil produces two pattern collections annually, designs for *Vogue Knitting International* and other publications, writes a feature column, "Ask Jil" in *Vogue Knitting's* magazine *Knit Simple*, and is busy with her tenth book. She lives in Maine with her husband, son, and Rexi-Martine, her Cock-a-Poo.

nina fuller

Nina Fuller is the one who so magically captures all these charming baby models digitally. A nationally acclaimed location and studio photographer, Nina has degrees from Silvermine College of Art and George Washington University in Photography, Painting and Printmaking. Location photography has been a creative focus for Nina, as well as photojournalism, as she trots from Great Britain to Australia on assignment for various publications, specializing in equine adventures. Her clients include LL Bean, Land's End, Horse & Hound, the Boston Globe and Atlantic Records. She lives in Maine with her two children on a bucolic horse farm. (www.ninafuller.net)

stephanie doben

Stephanie Doben is my studio assistant as well as pattern writer, technical pattern editor and a general knitting genius. She helps keep all the myriad balls in the air with calm aplomb and elegant intelligence. She is a delight to work with, sans doubt! Stephanie lives in Maine with her husband and son.

the knitters

My fabulous band of hand-knitters is the best on the planet! Knitting prototypes is always a tricky endeavor. Knitting under sharp deadlines can be an ordeal, but these garments have been perfectly done. Big thanks to Nita Young, Pam Tessier, Eroica Hunter, Stephanie Doben, Donna Michaud, Patti Waters, Joan Cassidy, and Noella Kingsley.

models

We shot this collection on location, which includes dragging equipment and lights from set to set. The bright lights are a bit daunting, and babies and toddlers jump in wide-eyed alarm. But Nina worked her magic once again, and we were able to capture the little imps in inimitable charm. Special thanks to all the wonderful parents who did their best at baby-wrangling at the photo shoots!

and more

Once again heartfelt thanks to my extraordinary publisher and editor, Anne Knudsen of Breckling Press, and to my gifted graphic designer, Maria Mann. Thanks to my beautiful mother, Nancy Whipple Lord, for teaching me to knit at the age of four, and to my lovely late grandmother Flora Hall Whipple for teaching my mother to knit. And loving thanks to my wonderful and brilliant husband David and my son Alexander for ideas, unending patience, continual understanding and support!

Knitting Market

The delicious yarns and products used in this book are available from the following distributors. You can always depend on these labels for yarns that are of the finest quality. Check their websites for shops in your area or for websites that carry their products online.

yarns

Berroco
14 Elmdale Road
PO Box 367
Uxbridge, MA 01569-0367
www.berroco.com
508-278-2527

Jil Eaton MinnowMerino by Classic Elite Yarns
125 Western Avenue
Lowell, MA 01851
www.classiceliteyarns.com

Manos Del Uruguay
Fairmont Fibers
915 N. 28th Street
Philadelphia, PA 19130
www.fairmontfibers.com

Rowan Yarns
Westminster Fibers, US Distributor
5 Northern Boulevard
Amherst, NH 03031
603-886-5041
www.knitrowan.com

Knit One Crochet Too
91 Tandberg Trail, Unit 6
Windham, ME 04062
www.knitonecrochettwo.com

needles

Addi Turbos from Skacel Collection, Inc.
224 SW 12th Street
Renton, WA 98055
213-854-2710

Palmwood Knitting Needles from Classic Elite Yarns
125 Western Avenue
Lowell, MA 01851
www.classiceliteyarns.com

buttons

Hand Made Fimo Buttons from Zecca
PO Box 215
North Egremont, MA 01252
860-435-2211
www.zecca.net

Central Yarn
569 Congress Street
Portland, ME 04101
207-775-0852
www.centralyarn.com

yf Yarn forward
yo Yarn over

Knitters' Abbreviations

approx	Approximately		pat (s)	Patterns(s)
beg	Beginning		psso	Pass the slipped stitch over the last stitch worked
CC	Contrasting color		rem	Remaining
cont	Continue(ing)s		rep	Repeat(s)
cn	Cable needle		rev St st	Reverse Stockinette Stitch, K all WS rows, P all RS rows
dec	Decrease(s)		rib	Rib(bing)
dpn	Double pointed needle		rnd(s)	Round(s) in circular knitting
est	Established		RS	Right side
inc (s	Increase(s)		sl	Slip(ed) (ping). Slip stitches from left hand needle to right hand needle
k	Knit			
k1 f&b	Knit into the front and back of each stitch		st(s)	Stitche(s)
k2tog	Knit two stitches together		ST st	Stockinette Stitch, K all RS rows, P all WS rows
MC	Main color			
p	Purl		tog	Together
p2tog	Purl two stitches together		WS	Wrong side

Needle Conversions

Metric (mm)	US	Old UK
2	0	14
2.25	1	13
2.5		
2.75	2	12
3		
3.25	3	10
3.5	4	
3.75		
5		
4	6	8
4.5	7	7
5	8	6
5.5	9	
6	10	4
6.5	10.5	3
7		2
7.5		1
8	11	0
9	13	00
10	15	000

AVON FREE PUBLIC LIBRARY

3 2529 11209 2689